The 91 Before Lindbergh

Peter Allen

Copyright © Peter Allen, 1984.

ISBN 0 906393 37 X

First published 1984
by Airlife Publishing Ltd.

Printed in England by Livesey Ltd., Shrewsbury.

Airlife Publishing Ltd.

7 St. John's Hill, Shrewsbury, England.

Contents

Foreword and Acknowledgements

The background of this book on early Transatlantic flying is, of course, furnished by other books and narratives. Although these works are numerous and many of them excellent, none seemed to me entirely satisfactory. Some were confined to the North Atlantic attempts, some omitted airships, others covered a single flight in great detail, some had too little background and some contained errors.

The more the subject was looked into, the more it appeared necessary to go back to the contemporary accounts or the flyers' own narratives to get to the truth. So, in the end, it seemed reasonable to put the story together once again as completely as possible to describe the conquest of the Atlantic, north and south, by aeroplane, airship, seaplane or flying boat, find the appropriate pictures, some commonplace but others never yet published, and while acknowledging the many accounts already available, looking at and quoting from what was written at the time. In doing this some fascinating matter came to light, unpublished before or lying dormant in files for fifty or sixty years and much of it in American, Spanish, Portuguese, French and Italian narratives of these great events. Visits to foreign museums also turned out to be well worthwhile.

Among the strange things that came to light was that the true number of pioneers who crossed the Atlantic by air before Lindbergh was difficult to pin down: how many people were aboard the Zeppelin LZ 126; did Major Franco fly with one, two or three companions; did the Brazilian *Jaú* arrive in time to be one of those who crossed before Lindbergh. Some myths have also been disposed of I hope: Whitten Brown did not walk on the Vimy's wings; the stowaway on the R34 was not court-martialled, nor did he weigh fourteen stone.

This book is not an attempt to denigrate Lindbergh; far from it, and the title is only intended to do justice to the many intrepid aviators who preceded or tried to precede him.

First and foremost among the sources to which I am indebted are the files of *Flight* and the *Aeroplane* the editors of which have turned up their volumes with admirable readiness. Their week-by-week accounts of events helped to keep the stories coherent. These journals have also permitted considerable verbatim quotation which gives, I think, liveliness to the story by using their items of news or editorial comment. Special articles too, such as General Maitland's diary of the flight of the airship R34, were valuable for reference. Next the newspaper coverage of these events as they occurred was studied; here the *Daily Mail,* the *Telegraph,* the *Illustrated London News,* the Spanish daily *ABC* and the *New York Times* have been drawn upon and quoted. The last of these has published an admirable summary of its reporting of flying in facsimile.

Great help has come from Mr Dignum of Associated Newspapers in providing suitable photographs. Helpful too was Mr Jack Bruce at the RAF Museum and especially so Mr John Bagley of the Science Museum who found for me unpublished matter about possible trans-Atlantic attempts during World War I, unpublished Handley Page material and let me have access to the Penn-Gaskell collection. In the USA the Smithsonian Institution readily turned up books and papers in their library at Washington and provided a treasure house of photographs to study and to use. The Canadian National Aviation Museum in Ottawa, the Portuguese Naval Museum and library in Lisbon and the Spanish Air Ministry and the Musée de l'Air in Paris all co-operated handsomely. Special help also came from Vickers in photographs of the Alcock and Brown flight. Mr Peter Berry, of the Atlantic Flying Control staff at Prestwick gave me some valuable background.

The detailed books dealing with individual attempts have, of course, been special sources of information. First of these is Lindbergh's own narrative *The Spirit of St Louis* written in 1953 long after the event, from which all other accounts of his crossing — and I think I have read seventeen in all — have sprung. From this work I have quoted about 500 words with the publisher's — Charles Scribner's Sons — approval. Most generously given was Sir Peter Masefield's permission to quote a valuable passage from the vote of thanks he gave in 1975 after John Grierson's lecture to the Royal Aeronautical Society on Lindbergh's flight.

Another account which has fathered many others is Alcock and Brown's own story which appears as the basis for Graham Wallace's book *The Flight of Alcock and Brown* (published by Putnam in 1955) and in *Our Transatlantic Flight* using their own words published by William Kimber in 1969.

Another invaluable work in this category is *First Across,* the story of the American flying boats by Richard K. Smith (published by Naval Institute Press in 1973). Other American works of special help were Grover Loening's *Take Off Into Greatness* 1968, excerpts from which are reprinted by G. P. Putnam's Son's permission and Lowell Thomas's *The First World Flight* (Houghton Mifflin 1925).

Nearer home I have found great support from Patrick Abbott's admirable book *Airship* (Adams & Dart 1973) and Kenneth Poolman's *Zeppelins over England* (Evans Bros. 1960), when dealing with airships, also Hans Knäusel's *Zeppelins and the USA* (Luftschiffbau Zeppelin 1976). Among European sources of special value were General Gomá Orduña's major work on the history of Spanish Aviation (Prensa Española 1945/51), *Cieli e Mari* by Cuponi (U. Mursia, 1973); helpfully the book *Gago Coutinho* and some private papers of the late General Correa, (head of the Portuguese Air Force) who wrote the book, were given to me by Mme. Correa. *L'Epopée de l'Atlantique Nord* published by Centre de Vulgarisation Aero-Astronautique 1961 and the French aviation journals *Icare* and *Pegase* were also most useful. Finally amongst the books special mention must be given to the late L. T. C. Rolt's *The Aeronauts* for the early balloon stories and Bob Dicker's account of the Alcock and Brown story from the ground staff side, some of which is reproduced by permission of the Transport Trust from *Transport Pioneers of the 20th Century* (Patrick Stephens 1981).

Peter Allen 1984

1.
Introduction: Lighter than Air

When one is sitting in Concorde at 55,000 feet above the Atlantic, idly watching the Mach-meter hovering around twice the speed of sound or the shadows on the window-frame marking the sun setting in the east, it is hard to imagine the ocean below, beset as nearly always by 'thick and wicked weather'.

It is hard too to remember that it is not yet sixty years since Lindbergh made the first flight in an aeroplane from mainland to mainland and only just sixty-five years since the Atlantic was crossed at all in flight. Perhaps strangest thought of all is that it is little more than eighty years since the Wright brothers left the earth in powered flight.

Perhaps the growth of the railway between 1825 and 1905 was similar to these developments but the technical transition from *Locomotion* of the Stockton & Darlington Railway with its primitive wagons to, say, the *Great Bear* of the Great Western or the fine steel cars just built for the *20th Century Limited* eighty years later shows fewer departures from the expected in power, speed, comfort and capacity for work than the abilities of Concorde or even a long-range Boeing 747 compared with the Wright *Flyer No. 1*.

Almost from the moment that man could leave the ground, even in uncontrollable balloons, the Atlantic has been a challenge, partly just 'because it was there', but somehow its conquest has had a much greater fascination than the conquest of the Pacific or the Indian Ocean. Lindbergh himself wrote: 'There is something unique about this ocean that gives it character above all other seas'. The reason is that the Atlantic has become the highway, the very centre of western civilisation, like the Mediterranean in its world two thousand years before.

Along the borders of the Atlantic for two hundred years have clustered the richest and most powerful nations of the earth with the poorer lands in Africa and South America waiting to be opened up to wealth and trade. Nearly three-quarters of the export trade of the free world originates from these countries; the greatest seaports in the world, the greatest airports are in these countries too. Today an average of over three hundred flights cross the Atlantic daily, with an annual total of eighteen million passengers aboard, and at peak times there are over forty flights an hour moving over the sea. Having been the busiest sea link in the world, now the Atlantic lies beneath the busiest air link. No wonder the desire to conquer it was so strong.

If you ask an American who was the first man to fly the Atlantic it is more than likely that he will say 'Lindbergh'. Well Lindbergh was first in a lot of things but not the first man to cross the Atlantic by air. He was in fact the 92nd. As an American friend said in illustration of the truth that you can't win them all: 'Take George Washington: first in the arts of war; first in the arts of peace; first in the hearts of his countrymen — and he married a widow'.

Just as it is now, Atlantic weather in those days was not only hostile but also unpredictable; high winds, rough seas, fog, rain, sleet, snow and icing conditions even in mid-summer were the rule and not the exception. Weather forecasting for more than the narrowest coastal waters was non-existent; all that could be relied upon then was the probability that there would be a following wind for a west to east flight on the North Atlantic and in the opposite direction south of the Equator, though for this to persist throughout the flight was unusual. If the weather was a constant anxiety so too were the instruments available to the flyers; proper compasses, blind-flying aids and reliable radios simply did not exist and navigation depended on dead reckoning or sextant readings, which were often unobtainable for hours on end. So pilots tended to overload themselves with fuel and many accidents were caused by this precaution.

If this was not bad enough, the aircraft were still primitive in the extreme. Ash, spruce, plywood, canvas and dope, bracing wires, open cockpits were the rule; the engines were heavy and unreliable with a poor power/weight ratio. The aircraft were just able to stagger across, propelling their own weight, their crew and a vast load of petrol. The Vickers Vimy of Alcock and Brown, now in the Science Museum in London, surprises you not by its smallness, for it is a fair size, but by its flimsiness.

Yet things improved so fast that the first payload was carried across the Atlantic as early as 1938 by means of the British Short-Mayo composite aircraft and a regular flying boat service was started just before and resumed immediately after World War II. What really clinched the matter was the air ferry which was started in the winter of 1940/41 by Donald Bennett, later of Pathfinder fame, between Britain, Canada, Newfoundland and the United States, bringing the planes over winter and summer for the war.

First in the field on this side was the great English balloonist Charles Green, who could attract huge crowds for his ascents from Vauxhall amid clouds of 'exasperated pyrotechnics' and who proposed an east to west flight as early as 1840,[1] flying low with a trail rope tied to copper floats and canvas buckets for replenishing

[1] See the late Tom Rolt's enjoyable book *The Aeronauts*.

his water ballast. It was lucky for him that this flight was never tried.

In America similar follies were being prepared. There seemed to be a widely held belief that there was a constant and steady west to east stream of air over the Atlantic which would waft a balloon over quite easily. A large transatlantic balloon called *Star of the West* was spoken of in 1835 and in 1843 'Professor' John Wise — all American aeronauts were professors — appealed to Congress, unsuccessfully,

Ascent of Mr. Green's balloon, London 1845. (Illustrated London News)

for funds to build a transatlantic balloon. In 1844 there was a famous hoax in a fictitious report of a balloon crossing written by Edgar Allan Poe. In 1859, however, Wise was able, with the support of A. O. Gager, to build a 50,000 cu. ft balloon called *Atlantic,* which however did not attempt it.

Also in 1859 another 'Professor', Thaddeus Lowe, built a huge balloon, the *Great Western* formerly the *City of New York,* of 725,000 cu. ft, with an estimated lift of $22\frac{1}{2}$ tons, a covered-in cabin and a 30 foot steam launch slung below with paddle wheels and an airscrew. Unable to get enough gas to inflate this monster in New

York, Lowe had to go to Philadelphia. Here in 1860 the balloon took off and got as far as the marshy flats of New Jersey, its arrival coinciding with that of Brunel's *Great Eastern* in New York. One more try by this balloon ended when it was caught in a squall and burst.

After the American Civil War, in which Wise's balloons towed by ships were used for observation, the American aeronauts were busy again. The *New York Times* in an editorial of 22 July 1873 wrote:

> 'Two or three projects for crossing to Europe by balloon are being discussed, and all are regarded by the public with incredulity. Since Prof. Lowe's mammoth airship the *City of New York* not only failed to cross the sea, but even to rise in the air at all, people have grown very sceptical'.

The article continued with a doubting tone but just avoided saying it was impossible to cross the Atlantic by balloon, only very difficult, pointing out that people had said that a steamship could not cross the ocean and that the electric telegraph was doomed to failure.

It is interesting to read in another article in the same issue of the *New York Times:* 'It is about twelve years ago since people began to grow vaguely alarmed over the prospect of British greatness and the British coal measures giving way about the same time.' But it concluded that readers need not worry.

Meanwhile Professor Wise was busy with another project, a large balloon of 600,000 cu. ft capacity built at the expense of the New York *Daily Illustrated Graphic,* with a two-storey enclosed cabin, auxiliary gas in balloons and a lifeboat. The press was far from optimistic about the outcome, saying:

> 'As the day approaches for Professor Wise to make his promised balloon ascent for a transatlantic trip the probabilities of success or failure are more and more critically considered. A measure of compassion also, we venture to add, is felt for the enterprising aeronaut, in apprehension not only of the failure of the attempt, but of the loss of life of a man whose daring and spirit of self sacrifice seem worthy of a better end than may await him. *(New York Times,* 11 August 1873)'

This scepticism was based, properly enough on the total lack of knowledge about the alleged west to east regular 'Trade Winds' across the Atlantic.

Professor Wise backed out of the *Daily Graphic* venture because he was not satisfied with the quality of the balloon that had been built; there had been tears in the cotton fabric of the envelope and the cabin had been abandoned, everything for the voyage being placed in the lifeboat which was secured to the gasbag. French

Walter Wellman owner of the airship 'America', with his engineer Melvin Vaniman, 1910.

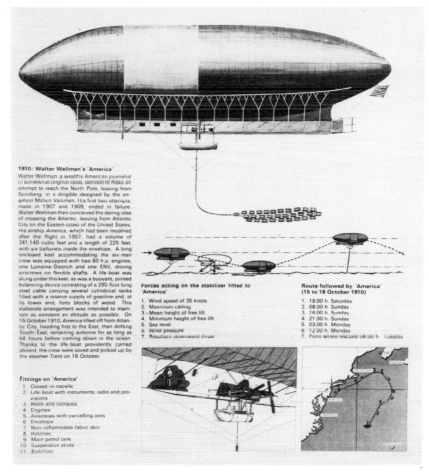

1910: Walter Wellman's 'America'

Walter Wellman, a wealthy American journalist of somewhat original ideas, decided to make an attempt to reach the North Pole, leaving from Spitzberg, in a dirigible designed by the engineer Melvin Vaniman. His first two attempts, made in 1907 and 1909, ended in failure. Walter Wellman then conceived the daring idea of crossing the Atlantic, leaving from Atlantic City on the Eastern coast of the United States. His airship *America*, which had been modified after the flight in 1907, had a volume of 341,140 cubic feet and a length of 225 feet, with six ballonets inside the envelope. A long enclosed keel accommodating the six-man crew was equipped with two 80 h.p. engines, one Lorraine-Dietrich and one ENV, driving airscrews on flexible shafts. A life-boat was slung under this keel, as was a buoyant, jointed balancing device consisting of a 295-foot long steel cable carrying several cylindrical tanks filled with a reserve supply of gasoline and, at its lower end, forty blocks of wood. This elaborate arrangement was intended to maintain as constant an altitude as possible. On 15 October 1910, *America* lifted off from Atlantic City, heading first to the East, then drifting South-East, remaining airborne for as long as 64 hours before coming down in the ocean. Thanks to the life-boat providently carried aboard, the crew were saved and picked up by the steamer *Trent* on 18 October.

Fittings on 'America'

1. Closed-in nacelle
2. Life-boat with instruments, radio and provisions
3. Helm and compass
4. Engines
5. Airscrews with swivelling axes
6. Envelope
7. Non-inflammable fabric skin
8. Hatches
9. Main petrol tank
10. Suspension struts
11. Stabilizer

Forces acting on the stabilizer fitted to 'America'

1. Wind speed of 35 knots
2. Maximum ceiling
3. Mean height of free lift
4. Minimum height of free lift
5. Sea level
6. Wind pressure
7. Resultant downward thrust

Route followed by 'America' (15 to 18 October 1910)

1. 18.00 h. Saturday
2. 08.00 h. Sunday
3. 16.00 h. Sunday
4. 21.00 h. Sunday
5. 03.00 h. Monday
6. 12.00 h. Monday
7. Point where rescued 08.00 h. Tuesday

Scale drawing of Wellman's airship. (*Airships*, published by Cassell 1971)

comment was: 'Wise qui avait dépassé la soixantaine, avait réfléchi et estimé que ce n'étaient plus des jeux de son age'[1]. What happened next day, 12 September 1873, was reported in the *New York Times* under the headline on page 1 'THE ROTTEN BALLOON' as follows:

'Twenty thousand spectators witnessed a great failure yesterday at the Capitoline Grounds. The *Daily Graphic* balloon fell to pieces for their entertainment, when about two-thirds filled with gas, and its collapse produced only laughter . . . They (the promoters) failed miserably, the "enterprize" fizzled out and the disgusted multitude was enraged at its own gullibility'.

When Professor Wise had refused, very sensibly, to fly in the balloon before the accident, his partner Professor Donaldson with two supporters, Mr Lund and Mr Alfred Ford, agreed to go and strutted importantly about until the cloth split and let the gas out and the public down.

[1]'Wise, who was over sixty, had pondered and concluded that he was too old for such games'. From *L'Epopée de L'Atlantique Nord*, 1961.

Incidently, the same issue of the *New York Times* reports Yellow Fever in the South with the words 'fearful ravages of the scourge in Louisiana — thirty-three deaths in one day — business at a standstill'. However, in an advertisement J. H. Schenck & Son were asserting that Schenck's Pulmonic Syrup, Schenck's Seaweed Tonic and Schenck's Mandrake Pills were the only medicines that would cure pulmonary consumption.

Donaldson, Lunt and Ford finally took off from New York for Europe in the repaired balloon on 6 October 1873, and after a four-hour flight came down near Canaan, Connecticut. The *New York Times* said:

'The descent of the aeronauts was not as graceful or nonchalant as their ascent. They were somewhat hurried. When near the ground Donaldson and Ford jumped out. Lunt followed and was caught like Absalom, in a tree. The guilty balloon escaped and had not been arrested at last account'.

Later, Donaldson and Wise both lost their lives in Lake Michigan, Donaldson in 1875 and Wise in 1879. Donaldson was accompanied by a journalist called Grimwood on a flight financed by Phineas T. Barnum.

These seem to be the last balloon attempts of the nineteenth century although Rolt records that Samuel King in 1881 built for the Atlantic a balloon said to have been of not less than a million cubic feet in volume, which flew but did not attempt the crossing, while *L'Epopée de L'Atlantique Nord* reports a fire balloon 700 feet long and 200 feet in diameter as under study by Rufus Gibbon Wells.

The next attempt, which was really the last of the primitive assaults, was made by Wellman's airship *America* in 1910, for although it was quite well found and well made by the standards of the day, it never really had a serious chance of flying the Atlantic. It made, however, the first attempt by a powered aircraft.

Walter Wellman, who was born in 1858, was a well-to-do journalist, newspaper proprietor, explorer and adventurer. He had taken part in two Polar expeditions, in 1894 and 1898, and organised another in 1906. For this he ordered an airship called the *America* designed by Louis Godard of Paris; this was delivered to Spitsbergen too late to try to fly to the North Pole that year. In 1907 they were back with an improved airship built by Wellman's engineer, Melvin Vaniman; this machine had a nominal range of over 2000 miles and carried 10 months' provisions in case of a forced landing as well as sleds and ten dogs. A trail rope called an 'Equilibrator' was fitted consisting of a long leather tube carrying stores. This attempt failed and so did another in 1909. This time the Equilibrator burst and the airship was able to come down close to Nansen's ship *Fram* which towed the *America* back to base, the envelope bursting *en route*. Wellman's polar airship was shown at the Olympia Aero Show of 1909 in some form.

Cramped quarters on board the airship 'America'.
(Illustrated London News)

Wellman's airship down and on the water, 1910. (Smithsonian Institution)

By 1910 the North Pole had been conquered by Admiral Peary but Wellman was ready for another adventure and with the backing of the *New York Times* and the London *Daily Telegraph* built another dirigible *America* using parts from his old ship; this was a semi-rigid with an enclosed keel which could accommodate six men. Below hung a lifeboat attached to which was the disastrous device the Equilibrator. This contraption consisted this time of 300 feet of steel cable to which were attached thirty cylinders, in three's; half of these carried the reserves of petrol for the airship and the rest were empty to give buoyancy. The idea was to keep the airship at an even height above the water; if it rose too far the drums would be dragged out of the water and their weight would pull the airship down again. No one seems to have thought of the effect of waves, which in the event imposed severe strains on the airship's structure and produced an atrocious tendency to seasickness.

If this were not enough, the airship was gravely under-powered with only two engines of a nominal 80 hp each and not even a pair; one a Lorraine-Dietrich and one an E.N.V. With a length of 225 feet and a volume of a little over 340,000 cubic feet Vaniman's airship was larger than the Goodyear blimps which fly around today and which use 350—400 hp.

Not only was the *America* under-powered but also under-rehearsed, for no trials whatever had been made when the intrepid aeronauts set out on Saturday, 15 October 1910, to fly the Atlantic. If this folly had been avoided the disastrous Equilibrator might have been disconnected. With four tons of petrol in the airship and

Imaginative Sketch of Wellman's rescue by the S.S. 'Trent' 1910.
(Science Museum)

another ton dragging in the sea, enough they hoped for the crossing for which they reckoned to take six to ten days, they left Atlantic City in a fog, towed by a small motor boat manned by the *Telegraph* correspondent and Wellman's son-in-law Chamberlin, so that the Equilibrator should not get tangled up with the rocky shore. The newsman wrote:

> 'We went slowly with the *America* trailing behind just as graceful as a swan and looking as we thought very weirdly picturesque as she came along moving very smoothly and responding easily but without a jerk to every movement of the hand which held the rope.

On board the airship were Walter Wellman, Melvin Vaniman the designer and engineer, assistant engineer Louis Loud, navigator Murray Simon (an Englishman, formerly a navigating officer of the White Star liner *Olympic*) and an Australian radio operator Jack

Irwin; Fred Aubert, a mechanic, went at the last moment because the Frenchman Jean Jacon declined: there was also a black cat.

'Up and across' was the cry of the crowd as Wellman stepped aboard 'Up for a trial', Mr Wellman called back, 'and only if the going's good up and over'.

The *Daily Telegraph* ran the following leading article on 17 October:

'One of the most adventurous journeys ever undertaken by brave men has just begun. The airship *America,* the second largest vessel of her type in the world, has left Atlantic City and is now — so we earnestly hope — speeding rapidly on her 3000 mile journey to England. She has set out to achieve the second conquest of the Atlantic — the first conquest of which must for ever stand to the credit of Columbus, for the names of the earlier heroes of the north who were blown across the sea by the mere sport of the winds have never been recorded — and her aim is to achieve it through the air, and not by ploughing through the waves . . .

The *America's* departure on Saturday had all the dramatic suddenness of a complete surprise. Her long wait of more than 20 days at Atlantic City had sorely tried the patience of her crew and, as our New York correspondent frankly states in his graphic account of the start, the American newspapers had already begun to accuse Mr. Wellman of 'blue funk' and to insinuate that he never intended to make the voyage at all . . .

Hurricanes apart the crucial problem with a great airship which has to face a 3000 mile journey across a waste of seas, when there is no chance of obtaining the slightest help in case of breakdown, is that of keeping her in the air by maintaining unimpaired the lifting power of

The Austrian airship 'Suchard', built in 1911 for an Atlantic attempt from Europe which did not come off. (Jane's Aircraft 1913)

the enormous gasbag . . . Hydrogen is one of the most elusive of gases. It searches unerringly for a way of escape and utilises passages which gases denser than itself could not detect'.

The New York correspondent of the *Telegraph* wrote:

'The departure from Atlantic City after 20 days of waiting for favourable weather conditions, and at a time when many people who had failed to realise the difficulties of the problems at stake were disappointed with the delays and explanations and were saying publicly that Mr. Wellman and Mr. Vaniman had built a machine of which, like Frankenstein's monster, they had become afraid and that not contrary winds on the transatlantic route nor gales off the New Jersey coast were responsible for the airship lingering here, but sheer funk, usually described by Americans as 'cold feet'.

Difficulties began almost at once with intermittent engine trouble. But even before that the terrified cat had made a disturbance by jumping overboard and had to be rescued by lowering a sack for it to grab. On the first evening in the fog they almost collided with a four-masted sailing ship and scared its crew half out of their wits. With one engine out of action and the airship labouring and buffeted by rising winds, Wellman reported that the Equilibrator was jerking the airship as it leapt from wave to wave and he ordered that the useless E.N.V. engine should be jettisoned, together with other inessentials, to lighten the ship. Having first progressed up the Atlantic coast as far as Nantucket contrary winds forced the airship south towards Bermuda. They were now drifting helplessly and on Tuesday morning, 18 October, decided to abandon ship. This was done and the crew entered their lifeboat with some difficulty as the Equilibrator had damaged it. They were exceedingly lucky to have met the SS *Trent* (Capt. C. E. Down) which saw their signals and picked them up, including the cat, about 400 miles east of the American coast after difficult manoeuvring lasting three hours. In all they had travelled about 1000 miles and been aloft for nearly 72 hours. The airship was abandoned at Lat. 35.43 and Long. 68.18.

On 19 October the *Telegraph* had this in its leader: 'Honour to the beaten. There will be universal regret that Mr Wellman's splendidly bold attempt to cross the Atlantic has ended in failure but universal congratulations that Fate has not exacted the supreme penalty'.

When interviewed ashore after rescue Wellman said that the Equilibrator had pulled hard, riding over the seas and shocking the ship. 'It set up a rolling motion which threatened total destruction . . . It was a dreadful night but the entire crew were calm and even cheerful. We were greatly exhausted'. He said that they had tried to make Bermuda keeping the engine for a last effort while they

*Vaniman's ill-fated airship 'Akron'
leaving its shed at Atlantic City
1912.* (Smithsonian Institution)

continued to jettison parts and superfluous weight to keep aloft.
The Equilibrator threatened to smash the lifeboat and struck it
during the critical launch: 'The Equilibrator was a fatal mistake'.
Simon was reported as the last man off the airship.

Wellman was full of praise for his crew and told newsmen that
young Aubert had managed to produce a wonderful dish of eggs
and bacon for all on board. At 8 p.m. the first night out near
Barnegat, New Jersey, they saw a schooner dead ahead in the fog;
they put the helm hard to starboard and just cleared her, 'our bilge
passing over her spanker and must have given the gang aboard the
deuce of a fright'. This was the fourmasted schooner *Addison E.
Bullard* (Capt. Sawyer) with a topmast of 110 feet above the sea. Her
captain said: 'Out of the darkness and mist shot a big aerial
phantom, as we imagined, going east and headed directly for the
Bullard. The thing was such a big surprise for all hands that we were
knocked off our pins . . . We could hear voices, some said the
airship scraped. But the airship had a perfect steering arrangement.
She came at us almost like the wind, and when almost on us she
turned suddenly, like a motor car shooting around a corner or a
short curve, and passed harmlessly out to sea. Wellman's last word
on the matter was: 'It was a trial worth making and we covered a
thousand miles over rough seas'. One leaves all this with the feeling
that Wellman was rather a good sort. He never flew again and lived
until 1934.

Vaniman's airship in flight just before it exploded.
(Smithsonian Institution)

Flight, in its issue of 26 February 1910, reported as follows:

'The plans of Herr Joseph Brucker, the Austrian aviator, for a trip across the Atlantic in a dirigible would appear to be progressing and Capt. Messner, who with Col. Schaeck won the Gordon Bennett balloon cup for Switzerland in 1908, is now associated with the scheme. It is proposed to start from Cadiz then to steer for Tenerife, from there to Porto Rico, then gradually beating back, sail over Havana, Cuba, New Orleans and so back to New York. In case of accident it was proposed that the nacelle of the dirigible should be a motor boat connected to either of two shafts; one for working the aerial propeller above the deck and the other a marine propeller, should it be necessary to come down on the surface of the ocean'.

This airship was built, being named *Suchard,* on 15 February 1911. It had one 110 hp N.A.G. engine in tandem with a 100 hp Escher, and a 4 hp auxiliary; the second engine was a spare. It was 199 ft long with a volume of 238,000 cu. ft and flew a number of times; it was given an enlarged gas bag but there is no record of it making a serious attempt on the Atlantic crossing, even from Tenerife. This was perhaps just as well as its speed was given in *Jane's* as only 17 mph.

Not content with the 1910 failure of Wellman's airship, Vaniman procured the building by F. A. Sieberling of Akron, Ohio, of a successor airship, the *Akron,* using the Goodyear Company's rubberised fabric, a large semi-rigid of 400,000 cu ft with an envelope 258 ft long. It was completed in September 1911. It had two 110 hp engines and one 80 hp engine with an auxiliary engine of 17 hp driving six propellers. The engines were fitted with carburettors which could be fed on hydrogen drawn from the ship's bulk. This may have been the cause of her loss or perhaps defective valves for releasing gas. Once again Atlantic City was the point of departure and on 2 July 1912, just as Vaniman and his three companions were airborne, the airship blew up and all on board perished.

The Atlantic was not crossed by a non-rigid airship until 1944 when six K-class blimps of US Naval Squadron No. 14 crossed in pairs to serve in the Mediterranean theatre of war. The first pair K123 and K130 left South Weymouth, Massachusetts, on 29 May

The first balloon to cross the Atlantic, 'Double Eagle II' of 1978. (Associated Newspapers)

1944 and flying via Newfoundland and the Azores reached Port Lyautey in Morocco on 1 June 1944.

After eighteen modern attempts to cross the Atlantic by free balloon, which cost the lives of six men and one woman, the helium-filled American *Double Eagle II* of Abruzzo, Anderson and Newman succeeded in crossing from Presque Isle, Maine to Evreux in France, a distance of 3600 miles in 139 hours and 6 minutes between 11 August and 17 August 1978. An earlier attempt a few weeks before by the British aeronauts Cameron and Davey in a helium/hot air balloon narrowly failed when they and their balloon *Zanussi* came down in the sea when only about 100 miles from the French coast.

2.
The Daily Mail Prize

Alfred Harmsworth, later Lord Northcliffe, revolutionised the British Press and changed the thinking and the attitudes of millions. The *Daily Mail* was something entirely new in London journalism and *The Times* under his ownership forsook the nineteenth century and entered the twentieth.

He had a genius for discerning what the British public wanted to read in a newspaper and selling it to them; he was farsighted, hard driving, authoritarian, mean, generous and successful. Most of his staff were afraid of him. He was intensely patriotic. All this led to great wealth and a press empire such as England had never seen before, entirely personal and autocratic, which fell to pieces immediately after his early death at the age of 57. Our society today no longer produces Napoleonic figures like this.

Northcliffe was greatly interested in new things and did much to encourage them. One of these was flying, which seized his imagination. So the *Daily Mail* put up many prizes for flying feats which look handsome even today; before World War I they must have seemed princely.

Lord Northcliffe inspecting the Wright biplane at Pau in 1909, with Kennedy Jones of the 'Mail'.
(Associated Newspapers)

As early as 1906, when nobody in Britain had left the ground in powered flight, the *Daily Mail* put up £10,000 — worth over £300,000 today — for the first flight from London to Manchester within 24 hours; and it is a measure of the farsightedness of the offer that it was not won until 1910, when the Frenchman Paulhan in a Blériot, chased by Britain's Claude Grahame-White, won it with a journey which included one stop. Those were the days when apart from the Wrights in the United States the best pilots and the best aeroplanes were French.

Then the *Daily Mail* in October 1908 offered £1000 for the first cross-Channel flight, which was won by Blériot on 25 July 1909, and followed this up by another £1000 prize for the first circular flight of a mile or more by a British pilot in a British-built machine. This was won on 30 October 1909 in a Short-Wright biplane with a 50 hp Green engine by young Moore-Brabazon (later Lord Brabazon of Tara), who held Britain's first pilot's certificate.

Next came the famous 1000 mile circuit of Britain in the hot summer of 1911, of personal recollection, for which the *Daily Mail* once more offered £10,000. This was won again by the French, Lt. Conneau ('Beaumont') in a Blériot narrowly beating Jules Vedrines in another Blériot on 26 July 1911 in a total flying time of 22 hours, 28 minutes. After that, in addition to a number of minor prizes, for example for the second cross-Channel flight, came a prize for a race around London known as the Aerial Derby, which was won by young Mr T. O. M. Sopwith in 1912. In 1913 £5000 was offered for a circuit of Britain by seaplane which was not won as the only starter, Harry Hawker, the Australian who was fast making a name for himself in Britain as a pilot, failed to complete the course.

After this came the astounding offer on 1 April 1913 of a *Daily Mail* prize of £10,000 for the first transatlantic flight. This was to be won by the first aviator who crossed the Atlantic in an aeroplane from any point in Great Britain or Ireland to any point in Newfoundland, Canada, or the United States, in 72 consecutive hours, flying in either direction. The prize was open to pilots and machines of all nationalities. Only one machine was allowed per attempt but it could make an intermediate stop or stops on water without penalty; towing was allowed but if the pilot boarded a ship he had to resume flying from where he left his aircraft. The start and finish could be made from land or water but the pilot had to cross the coastline at each end. It is evident from the rules that airships were excluded and that it was expected that flying boats or floatplanes would be used.

This farsighted offer was naturally greeted with disapproval or derision in many quarters. Sir Philip Burne Jones wrote to the *Daily Mail* that their offer of £10,000 for flying the Atlantic was 'an inducement to suicide' while *Punch,* always ready with reactionary ridicule, replied to an earlier offer by 'putting up' £30,000, one-third to go to the first aeronaut to go to Mars and back in a week, one-

Gustav Hamel, an early contender for the 'Daily Mail' prize, who was lost at sea in May 1914.
(Associated Newspapers)

Princess Löwenstein-Wertheim under instruction in 1914. She was hoping to fly the Atlantic in 1914 and perished in a later attempt in 1927.

(Associated Newspapers)

third for the first person to reach the centre of the earth in a fortnight and one-third for the first person to swim the Atlantic.

In aviation circles the *Daily Mail* offer was taken seriously and first reports in 1913 stated that entries had been made by Herr Rumpler and Mr E. C. Gordon England, a well-known British flyer who later became renowned as a large man driving small sports and racing cars at Brooklands and elsewhere with fabric-covered bodies of his own design. There was also mention of entries from M. Louis Blériot, M. Wynmalen of Belgium and Colonel Cody. Roland Garros, Marc Pourpe and Brindejonc des Moulnais of France, and Enea Bossi in Italy were reported to have said they would enter[1]. There was talk too of a young German designer called Dornier. An American called Jack McGee announced that he proposed to start on the 4 July from Newport, Rhode Island, in a Burgess-Wright waterplane. None of these came to anything, however, and 1913 merged into 1914; by that Spring though there were two firm entries from Gustav Hamel, as pilot for Mr Mackay Edgar's Martinsyde monoplane, and from Lt. J. C. Porte, RN (retired), as pilot for Mr Rodman Wanamaker's Curtiss flying boat *America*. There were rumours too that Mr A. V. Roe in England was going to build a three-seater AVRO capable of 70 mph to compete for the prize, and Her Serene Highness Princess Löwenstein-Wertheim was having a biplane built by Handley Page with the intention of competing.

Gustav Hamel was one of the first British pilots to make a name and with his youthful good looks soon became something of a hero. He was born in June 1889, the son of a well-known Harley Street

[1] See Richard K. Smith's book *First Across,* Naval Institute Press, 1973.

Lt. Commander J. C. Porte, Britain's leading flying-boat designer. (Associated Newspapers)

doctor of Scandinavian origin. The young man obtained a French pilot's certificate on 3 February 1911 in a Morane and the British certificate on 14 February in a Blériot. He did well in numerous races, was second to young Tom Sopwith in the Aerial Derby in 1912 and won it in 1913. He was twice commanded by King George V to loop the loop. His Martinsyde Atlantic was a monoplane 45 ft long with 65 ft wingspan, driven by a 215 hp Sunbeam engine; it had a disposable undercarriage and was fitted with two bulkheads in the fuselage to help flotation and a telescopic mast from which a distress signal could be flown. Apart from an artist's sketch of Hamel's Atlantic plane and an outline drawing of it in *The Aeroplane,* pictures of this machine have not come to light. Hamel's sponsor, Mackay Edgar, was a wealthy Scottish-Canadian capitalist who enjoyed motor sport. He was the owner of a series of fast motor boats, on one of which, the *Maple Leaf IV* Sopwith, who was becoming famous as a flier of aeroplanes, won back the International Motor Boat championship for the Harmsworth Trophy from the Americans in 1912 and retained it over here in 1913.

The Martinsyde challenge came to nothing because Hamel was lost in the Channel on 23 May 1914, bound for England and flying a new Morane monoplane with an 80 hp Gnome mono-soupape engine. He had left Villacoublay in France at 4.40 a.m. and stopped twice *en route* as his engine was giving trouble. He left Hardelot at 12.15 p.m. in poor weather and was never seen again. No trace was ever found and the King sent his condolences to Dr Hamel. Death was presumed on 9 September 1914, but such was the anti-German hysteria of that period that disgraceful rumours circulated that Gustav Hamel had defected to the enemy.

More is known about the other Atlantic contender of 1914. Mr Rodman Wanamaker, the owner of the famous department store in Philadelphia, wished to commemorate the 100th anniversary of the signing of the Treaty of Ghent in 1815, which set the seal on a century of peace between the United States and Britain. In order to do this fittingly and to gain publicity for his business he commissioned Glenn H. Curtiss to build a large flying boat to serve as his gesture of goodwill and compete for the prize.

Glenn Curtiss started as a cycle and motorcycle racer, then became the world pioneer of practical flying boats and indeed second only to the Wright brothers in American aviation history. The competition between the Wright brothers and the other potential American manufacturers, particularly Curtiss, had, it can be argued, a considerable effect of the development of the aircraft industry of the United States and certainly it makes interesting reading. Many of the complications and misunderstandings which arose assuredly sprang from the Wrights' extraordinary reticence and cool assurance. Lord Northcliffe, who saw Wilbur Wright's display at Pau in France in 1909, called it 'a miracle' and described the pilot as a 'very taciturn, hermitlike, frugal man' who would not fly on Sundays. Their work with gliders from 1899 on and then their first powered flights from December 1903 through 1904 and 1905 with the Flyers No. 1, No. 2 and No. 3 showed that they had mastered the crucial problem of stability in flight by means of a curved wing surface and by distorting or warping the wingtips which imparted lateral control in turning. This was a major invention, and a master patent evolved from it. For not only did their patent protect the wing warping design which their aircraft used, but also movable pieces on the wingtips — ailerons — which others were quick to see produced the same effect.

The Wrights's experimental flying in 1904 and 1905 attracted little attention in the United States, and next to none in Europe, where a ludicrous flight of 82 feet by Santos Dumont in October 1906 in an absurd, tail-first boxkite was hailed as man's first powered flight, which moreover won the Archdeacon Prize of the French Aero Club of 4000 francs. No one seemed to have heard of the Wrights, who had ended 1905 with a flight of 24 miles in 28 minutes months before anyone in Europe had left the ground at all. They continued to live quietly sitting on their patent of 1906 and trying to interest the US Government in their invention. They had approached the US Army, through their Congressman, in January 1905 with the data of the 104 flights they had made the year before, including two of five minutes with controlled turns and speeds up to 35 mph. It will be no surprise to learn that no interest was shown. There were also abortive talks with the British in 1905 and the French in 1906. Finally the US Army, after months of dickering, ordered a Model A Wright Flyer in February 1908.

Glenn Curtiss, the American flying-boat pioneer. He was also an early motorcycle racer. (National Motor Museum)

World's Record – Ormond Beach, Fla.
1 Mile – 26 2/5 Seconds.
8 Cylinder, 40 H.P. Motor Cycle
Built by The Curtiss Manufacturing Company, Hammondsport, N.Y.

All this while the Wrights, totally self-possessed, went quietly on with their patient negotiating and, what is an astounding fact, they did not fly *at all* in 1906 and 1907. Then in 1908, with the US Army order at last secured, they proceeded to astonish the world.

In the summer before Henri Farman, an Englishman resident in France, won the Deutsch de la Muerthe prize of 10,000 francs by making the first circular flight in Europe of one kilometre in a Voisin biplane. France was hailed as the fatherland of flight and the Wrights put down as bluffers.

Then in August 1908 Wilbur Wright set up shop in Le Mans and, as Grover Loening wrote: 'As soon as he started to fly, all the world knew and the French in particular knew that the stories and rumours about the Wrights were true . . . The pathetic struggles, short hops and turns of Voisin, Farman, Delagrange, Santos Dumont and Ferber were then appraised as childish performances compared to what Wilbur Wright proceeded to show them about flying'[1].

Scepticism was replaced by wild adulation. Wilbur Wright won several prizes and flew non-stop on one occasion for two hours and twenty minutes. The Wrights were supreme.

They were not only supreme as flyers but also protected by impregnable patents which threatened to reduce all competition, at any rate in the United States, to impotence or tribute, for the Wrights, with Wall Street backing, were ready to protect themselves. Alexander Graham Bell, the inventor of the telephone, set up an aircraft firm, the Aerial Experiment Association, with Glenn H. Curtiss in 1908 and immediately a patent row blew up over movable wingtips on the prizewinning *June Bug* which Curtiss built. The Wrights contended here that they had imparted one of their secrets, namely the unexpected movement of the centre of pressure on a curved wing section in flight, to one of Bell's partners, Selfridge, for experimental purposes only and not for commercial use. Ironically Lt. Selfridge was the first American to be killed in an air accident when flying with Orville Wright in 1908.

Curtiss started out on his own in 1909 and proceeded to make and sell aeroplanes fitted with ailerons for lateral control. Curtiss and the Wrights were in contention all through 1909, 1910 and 1911, both in flying and in litigation. At the Belmont Park meeting in October 1910 and at other flying meetings in the United States the Wrights collected royalties from Curtiss and all the contestants, or from the promoters, even Britain's Grahame-White who won the Gordon Bennett Speed Trophy Race. In 1910 the Wrights obtained injunctions against Paulhan and Henri Farman in the US, winning finally in the Appeal Court at Buffalo in July 1913. New rivals were appearing on the US scene, such as Glenn Martin, and the Wright patent hung like a cloud over all, claiming a royalty of 20 per cent of the profits on all planes sold.

[1]Grover Loening *Take-off Into Greatness*. Putnam, 1968.

Miss Katherin Masson launching the flying-boat 'America' in 1914. Lt. Commander Porte is on the left.
(Canadian National Aviation Museum)

Later a discreditable attempt was made to get round the Wrights' unpopular monopoly by resurrecting the Langley flyer, called the *Aerodrome,* of 1903 and surreptitiously altering it to make it capable of flight and so pre-date the Wrights's patents. Thirty-five changes were made to the *Aerodrome* and this 1914 model did make a five-second jump in May 1914. This monstrous hoax, to which the Smithsonian Institution was a party, was only relegated to its proper place in 1947, when the Wright Flyer was returned from the Science Museum in London to Washington.

Not only did the Wrights become very rich but also it must be feared a little smug. Wilbur, in a patent suit, gave forth.

'And yet it is in such capricious, wilful, spasmodic and withal powerful a medium as this that our Wright flying machine rides and speeds away with man or men aboard like a veritable living albatross. It plants itself on the incorrigible air and rides upon its very incorrigibility[1]'.

Wilbur Wright, who was the elder of the two, died of typhoid in 1912 aged 45, and Orville, who was not the commercial brain of the group, retired more and more into research in the background; he sold his company very satisfactorily and ceased to be a factor in the industry. He died in January 1948 at the age of 77.

The Wright stranglehold was settled finally by the setting up of a patent pool in 1917, but there seems to be little doubt that the monopoly must have been a real handicap to the early growth of the US aircraft industry and one of the principal reasons for its relatively poor showing in World War I and for some years

[1] Grover Leoning quoting Wilbur Wright.

The flying-boat 'America' on Keuka Lake, 1914. (Canadian National Aviation Museum)

afterwards. The last time that the Wright patents were used to any effect was in 1919 when they successfully put a stop to a plan to import and dump surplus war-planes from Britain, which would have threatened to destroy the American aircraft industry.

It was also a handicap that the basic Wright aeroplane design, which with its pusher airscrews had severe limitations, was overtaken and superseded by more modern ideas so that the conventional tractor type of aeroplane of World War I and of the twenties and thirties evolved into something different from the original history-making Wright flyers. But while the US aircraft industry was unable to produce a combat aeroplane, before the end of the War it did produce a first-class aeroplane engine, the Liberty 12-cylinder water-cooled V-twin of 300 hp rising to 400/425 hp. This was basically a Packard Motors' design.

To return to the *Daily Mail* prize, Rodman Wanamaker naturally turned to Glenn Curtiss not only as the number two American designer but as the number one flying-boat man. He had already built a number of successful flying-boats and was eager to design a bigger craft with a chance to beat the Atlantic. Wanamaker was willing to spend $25,000.

The first plan was for a single-engined flying-boat with a 200 hp Curtiss motor, but this was soon abandoned in favour of a big twin-engined flying-boat, the *America,* which was built at Hammondsport on Keuka Lake in the attractive Finger Lakes district of upper New York State. Curtiss was joined in the early stages by Lt. John H. Towers USN, whom he had taught to fly. They expected to be the crew of the *America* but Curtiss's wife had persuaded him to fly less, so that Towers and another US naval officer became the proposed crew. This, however, the US Navy Department would not allow. There was war on the Mexican border and naval officers who could fly were wanted down south; Towers was out.

So Lt. Porte from Britain, who was well-known to Curtiss as he had shipped a Curtiss flying-boat over to England, was invited to help to test and fly the machine, and it was intended that he should be accompanied by an officer of the US Navy, George Hallett, on the Atlantic attempt.

Cyril John Porte was an Irishman born at Bandon in County Cork in February 1884. He joined the Navy and became one of the first submariners. He was invalided out of this service with incipient tuberculosis and joined the Royal Naval Air Service, where he learned to fly in 1910. He became interested in flying boats working with the well-known boat builders S. Saunders of Cowes.

The *America,* which followed an established Curtiss design, was a twin-engined biplane with unequal span, the upper wing being 74 ft across and the lower 45 ft. The boat body was enclosed and had space to sleep behind the two seats. The body was 30 ft long and the all-up weight was 5000 lb. The power plant consisted of two 100 hp water-cooled Curtiss O.X. engines mounted between the wings on either side of the body and driving pusher screws.

First tests on Keuka Lake were apparently promising for there

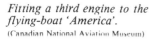

Fitting a third engine to the flying-boat 'America'.
(Canadian National Aviation Museum)

was a report that a start from Newfoundland to fly direct to Ireland, some 1850 miles, would be made on 15 or 16 July 1914. However, difficulties arose with taking off with full load and a second flight plan was adopted for mid-August, which re-routed the flight via the Azores, to cut down the long non-stop section to Ireland, to be followed by a 'leg' to the coast of Spain near Vigo, thence on a straight line past Ushant to Plymouth.

More snags developed and a report in *Flight* for 31 July 1914 spoke of several alterations being needed, including the fitting of a third engine to enable the flying-boat to take off with full load and the rebuilding of the hull, which would have postponed the attempt until October. The alterations were apparently not too successful and it began to look as if the *America* was not good enough for the passage. A second flying-boat was also built as a back-up.

However, before that date the German armies were on the march and the *Daily Mail* withdrew its prize offer 'for the duration'.

The outbreak of war also put a stop to Princess Löwenstein-Wertheim's venture with the Handley Page L/200, a single-engined biplane with a 60 ft span.[1]. The quotation for the plane was £3,000 and she placed an order with Handley Page on 1 May for this sum, with the stipulation that it be ready in three months. There were two seats side-by-side in an enclosed cabin with a third seat for resting. The plane was to be fitted with floats. The engine was to be a 200 hp Canton-Unne water-cooled radial built by Salmson in France. The engine only arrived after the war had started and the Admiralty commandeered it, so the L/200 never flew. There were arguments about return of the money paid but it was believed that she got her money back.[2] The intrepid princess, who was born Lady Anne Savile, was a daughter of the Earl of Mexborough and widow of a German nobleman who had been killed in 1899 fighting for Spain in the Spanish-American war. She had another go at the Atlantic, however, in 1927 when sixty years old. With two pilots, Minchin and Hamilton, she left Upavon on 31 August, bound for Ottawa, in a single-engined Fokker monoplane *St Raphael.* They were never seen again though the plane was said to have been sighted by a tanker in mid-Atlantic.

Although Wanamaker's *America* never flew the Atlantic, it did cross it as it was sold to Britain and came over in the *Mauretania.* This aircraft, which developed in its home country into the H12, the large America flying boat, was the true forerunner not only of all later World War I American but also British flying boats, and Porte contributed greatly to this development work, although he was not enamoured of the plywood and fabric parts in the boat bodies of the original design as it meant that they could not operate in rough weather. Not only did Porte supervise the construction of the British-built H12 flying-boats with two 275 hp Rolls-Royce Eagle

[1]See Ch. Barnes's book on the Handley Page Company.
[2]According to Mr John Bagley of the Science Museum who provided this information.

Imaginative drawing of Hamel's
'Martinsyde'. (Flight)

engines, but he was part designer of the F1, F2, F3 and F5 improved flying-boats derived from the H12 and, like it, tractor biplanes, built by firms like Doulton and Paul of Norwich, woodworkers and builders of furniture. The series of Porte flying-boats culminated in a monster five-engined triplane, the F4, called the *Felixstowe Fury,* which was built in 1918 and was at one time the biggest plane in the world.

The *Felixstowe Fury* had a span of 123 ft on its two upper wings and a length of 60 ft. Powered by five Rolls-Royce Eagle VII engines of 344 hp, it weighed in at 33,400 lb. On one test flight it carried 24 passengers, 5000 lb of ballast and fuel for seven hours. Clearly this could have been a contender for the Atlantic prize but it crashed on test in 1919 off Plymouth with two deaths.

Porte himself barely survived the war; although a dying man, he had worked furiously hard not only as a designer but also as a pilot, going on bombing raids on the enemy coast and taking part in the first experiment in which one aircraft bore another into the air and then cast off the upper plane to fly alone. This took place in May 1916 when Porte in one of his big flying-boats took off from Felixstowe with a Bristol Scout on his upper mainplane. At 1000 ft Lt. Day switched on his engine, released the clamps holding him and flew away safely to Martlesham Heath. In the summer of 1919 John Porte, by then a Lieutenant Colonel (Wing Commander) in the RAF and a CMG, had just been able to greet the American flying-boat crew which was the first across the Atlantic before he succumbed to tuberculosis and died at the age of 36. The late Sir Walter Raleigh, the first official historian of the RAF, wrote: 'The shortest possible list of those who served the country in the hour of need would have to include his name'. For a time a BEA airliner was named after him.

3.
1919: The Great Year

Before the war ended the *Daily Mail* announced that they would renew their offer of £10,000 for the first crossing of the Atlantic by aeroplane and on 14 November 1918, immediately after the Armistice, they did so.

The rules first announced were the same as those laid down in 1913 but an amendment was made on 1 February 1919 by which aircraft and pilots of enemy origin were excluded. Lord Northcliffe was no friend of Germany and for a long-range German bomber to have won the prize would have been intolerable. In the US Navy's popular account of their successful crossing of the Atlantic by flying boat in 1919, and elsewhere it is stated that the new rules prohibited 'ocean stoppages', thus eliminating the Americans, but this is untrue.

It is surprising that the Atlantic had not been flown during the war, for aircraft had developed fast: bigger structures, more powerful and reliable engines, better power-weight ratios and better controllability; though compared with today's expensive monsters, they were still flimsy, vulnerable creatures of wood and fabric, cheap and quick to build, repair or modify. The instruments by

The Fairey IIIC 'Transatlantic'.
(Canadian National Aviation Museum)

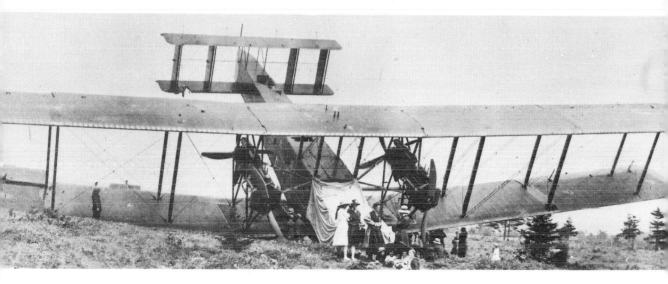

*Handley Page V1500 after crash
at Parrsboro*
(Canadian National Aviation Museum)

*Handley Page flying over Long
Island.* (Canadian National Aviation Museum)

today's standards and the radio and meteorological aids were still
extremely poor. While the Felixstowe team was busy with bigger
and better flying boats, urged on by the submarine menace, so too
were their comrades at Curtiss in the USA, and by 1917 work had
started in the United States on the design of a big anti-submarine
flying boat of unorthodox type, to be capable of flying the Atlantic.
The story of these NC — Navy-Curtiss — boats comes in the next
chapter so they can be left here with the note that the British mission
to the USA in 1918 was not impressed by them.

The Science Museum[1] has been kind enough to draw attention to

[1] In the person of Mr John H. Bagley, who has allowed the use of his unpublished notes on the
subject.

Handley Page V1500 with its crew. Left to right: Brackley, Kerr, Gran and Wyatt.
(Canadian National Aviation Museum)

a Handley Page proposal for a transatlantic flight during the War. In October 1917 Handley Page suggested to Sir William (later Lord) Weir, the Director-General of Aircraft Production at the Ministry of Munitions, that a flight across the Atlantic by one of his twin-engined 0/400 bombers, suitably modified, would be good for morale in the new RAF, and in Britain generally, and would dismay the enemy who would then know that no part of their territory would in future be out of range. Handley Page also believed that the Italians were considering such a flight by a Caproni Ca5 heavy bomber which was a rival for the equipping of a possible US heavy bomber force.

Handley Page's calculation claimed that an 0/400 stripped of armament and fitted with extra tanks could carry fuel for 27 hours in the air or 2150 miles at cruising speed. This they said would allow a flight from Newfoundland to Ireland with a margin of safety. Unfortunately they mixed up statute miles with nautical miles and it was then agreed that the margin of safety was not enough.

So then the alternative of flying via the Azores was taken up, as by this time — early 1918 — large orders had been placed for American-built 0/400 bombers, which were to be shipped over in parts and assembled at a new factory in Oldham. The possibility of flying over completed machines was obviously attractive.

The news got out; other proposals came up and were vetoed, including one from Vickers to fly a Vimy across and another from

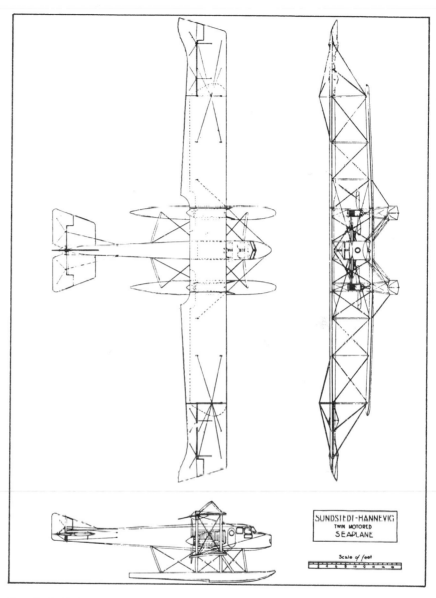

SUNDSTEDT-HANNEVIG
TWIN MOTORED
SEAPLANE

Drawing of Sundstedt-Hannevig seaplane.
(Jane's *Aircraft* 1919)

Lt. Col. John Porte (as he had become with a new RAF rank) to fly over in a Felixstowe F-5 twin-engined flying boat, which the Americans had adopted. Indeed the Americans were themselves considering the possibility of flying their version of this flying-boat, the F-5L, to the European theatre via the Azores.

Calculations on the feasibility of an 0/400 flight were made at the Air Ministry by Ogilvie, the head of the Technical Department of the Air Board, aided by two scientific Majors, Tizard and G. I. Taylor, who later became Professors, Knights, and Fellows of the Royal Society. The conclusion was reached that the project was possible if a radio guidance system was installed at the Azores.

So a start was made to find suitable landing grounds in

Newfoundland and the Azores. In Newfoundland, Lt. Everson and later Capt. Reid picked out as suitable Glendinning's Field at Mount Pearl near St. John's and some work was done on it. The war ended, interest lapsed and the Newfoundland Government declined an offer of this airfield as a permanent aerodrome. However it came into use by the Sopwith team for their transatlantic attempt in May 1919.

A wartime crossing by German Zeppelin would have been possible. A remarkable flight had been achieved in 1917 by the modified naval Zeppelin L59 with her gas capacity increased to $2\frac{1}{2}$ million cubic feet. This was an attempt to reach and supply von Lettow-Vorbeck's troops still holding out in German East Africa. The airship left Yamboli in Bulgaria, but early on the second day, when already past Khartoum and over 2000 miles out, she was recalled, one report being that this was engineered by British Intelligence. So L59 was turned around and 96 hours and 4200 miles after departure was back at base, moreover with fuel for another 3000 miles on board. Right at the end of the war, a proposal was discussed for sending the L72 on a bombing raid on New York, or at least as a demonstration and a propaganda act of defiance. The L71 was prepared for a similar foray as far west across the USA as it could get. Largely by the efforts of Dr Eckener, who had succeeded to the leadership of the firm on the death of Count Zeppelin in 1917, these provocative flights were not carried out.

So in 1919 all was poised for an assault on the Atlantic and the year indeed turned out to be an *annus mirabilis*. The American flying boat team was first across, Hawker and Mackenzie Grieve gave the British public a glorious failure to applaud, Alcock and Whitten

Sundstedt-Hannevig seaplane under construction.
(Jane's *Aircraft* 1919)

Royal Aero Club of the United Kingdom,
3, CLIFFORD STREET, LONDON, W. 1.

Telegraphic Address : "Aerodom, London."
Telephone : Regent 1327-8-9.

"DAILY MAIL" £10,000 PRIZE.
Cross-Atlantic Flight.

(Under the Competition Rules of the Royal Aero Club.)

The Proprietors of the "Daily Mail" have offered the sum of £10,000 to be awarded to the aviator who shall first cross the Atlantic in an aeroplane in flight from any point in the United States, Canada, or Newfoundland to any point in Great Britain or Ireland, in 72 consecutive hours. (The flight may be made either way across the Atlantic.)

Qualification of Competitors.—The competition is open to persons of any nationality not of enemy origin, holding an Aviator's Certificate issued by the International Aeronautical Federation and duly entered on the Competitors' Register of the Royal Aero Club.

No aeroplane of enemy origin or manufacture may be used.

Entries.—The Entry Form, which must be accompanied by the Entrance Fee of £100, must be sent to the Secretary of the Royal Aero Club, 3, Clifford Street, London, W. 1, at least 14 days before the entrant makes his first attempt.

No part of the Entrance Fee is to be received by the *Daily Mail*. All amounts received will be applied towards payment of the expenses of the Royal Aero Club in conducting the competition. Any balance not so expended will be refunded to the competitor.

Starting Place.—Competitors must advise the Royal Aero Club of the starting place selected, and should indicate as nearly as possible the proposed landing place.

All starts must be made under the supervision of an Official or Officials appointed by the Royal Aero Club.

Identification of Aircraft.—Only one aircraft may be used for each attempt. It may be repaired en route. It will be so marked before starting that it can be identified on reaching the other side.

Stoppages.—Any intermediate stoppages may only be made on the water.

Towing.—Towing is not prohibited.

Start and Finish.—The start may be made from land or water, but in the latter case the competitor must cross the coast line in flight. The time will be taken from the moment of leaving the land or crossing the coast line.

The finish may be made on land or water. The time will be taken at the moment of crossing the coast line in flight or touching land.

If the pilot has at any time to leave the aircraft and board a ship, he must resume his flight from approximately the same point at which he went on board.

GENERAL.

1. A competitor, by entering, thereby agrees that he is bound by the Regulations herein contained or to be hereafter issued in connection with this competition.

2. The interpretation of these regulations or of any to be hereafter issued shall rest entirely with the Royal Aero Club.

3. The competitor shall be solely responsible to the officials for the due observance of these regulations, and shall be the person with whom the officials will deal in respect thereof, or of any other question arising out of this competition.

4. A competitor, by entering, waives any right of action against the Royal Aero Club or the Proprietors of the *Daily Mail* for any damages sustained by him in consequence of any act or omission on the part of the officials of the Royal Aero Club or the Proprietors of the *Daily Mail* or their representatives or servants or any fellow competitor.

5. The aircraft shall at all times be at the risk in all respects of the competitor, who shall be deemed by entry to agree to waive all claim for injury either to himself, or his passenger, or his aircraft, or his employees or workmen, and to assume all liability for damage to third parties or their property, and to indemnify the Royal Aero Club and the Proprietors of the *Daily Mail* in respect thereof.

6. The Committee of the Royal Aero Club reserves to itself the right, with the consent of the Proprietors of the *Daily Mail*, to add to, amend or omit any of these rules should it think fit.

Published conditions of 'Daily Mail' prize. (Flight)

1st February, 1919.

For Entry Form, see over.

Starting the Short Shirl, 'Shamrock'. (BBC/Hulton)

Brown won the *Daily Mail* prize and the British airship R34 made the first east to west crossing and the first round trip.

That Britain should have claimed a major share of these honours was not surprising. At the end of the war, she stood on a pinnacle of power and strength which is unimaginable today. In spite of fighting from the first day to the last and suffering two and three-quarter million casualties, with nearly 700,000 dead, on the Western front alone, in spite of the abominable losses at Passchendaele in 1917 and 400,000 casualties in the furious German assaults in their last desperate offensives in 1918, it was an army largely of Imperial soldiers which inflicted on 8 August 1918 the Black Day of the German Army, which convinced Ludendorff and the Kaiser that the war was lost.

When the war ended, with 60 Divisions of Imperial troops in France and a million soldiers in other theatres — over $3\frac{1}{2}$ million in all in the various armies — a total of six million men were under arms. The Grand Fleet had reached a total of 4000 vessels, had beaten the submarine menace and supported a merchant marine of 20,000 ships. It had reduced the once proud German Navy to a state where it could no longer be trusted to put to sea, and at the surrender of the German fleet after the Armistice it enjoyed but did not need the presence of French and American squadrons.

In aviation the Empire was equally powerful. At the end of the war, over 347,000 people were employed in the British aircraft industry, three times as many as in Germany and twice as many as in France. The RAF possessed 22,647 aeroplanes, 103 airships and nearly 700 aerodromes.[1] While these aircraft, which included such experimental improbabilities as quadruplanes, the *Felixstowe Fury* and the huge Tarrant triplane, had little significance for any peacetime use that could then be imagined, there is little doubt that Britain came out of World War I with 'the means to match our maritime achievements by making ourselves the greatest civil aviation power in the world'.[1] Certainly the Civil Air Transport Committee, set up under Lord Northcliffe's chairmanship in 1917, thought so, though their report pointed out the need to subsidise the industry to enable it to develop. H. G. Wells — whose masterly *War in the Air* of 1907 makes splendid reading even today — was a member of Northcliffe's Committee; he wrote: 'A people who will not stand up to the necessity of Air Service planned on a World Scale and taking over thousands of aeroplanes and thousands of men from the very onset of peace has no business to pretend to anything more than (a) Second-rate position in the World. We cannot be both Imperial and mean . . .'

The Alliance 'Seabird'.
(Real Photo/Ian Allan)

Sir Sefton Brancker writing in the 'Golden Peace' issue of the *Daily Mail* said: 'The War has bequeathed to us as a nation a great heritage in the air. Our pilots are the best, our designs the most efficient, and our industry the greatest in the world. Supremacy in the air is ours for the making.' Alas how differently it turned out.

Certainly the Americans, who were then organising a massive transatlantic naval exercise, thought so. Their naval 'Trans-Atlantic

[1] *The Water Jump* by David Beaty. Secker & Warburg. 1976.

Flight Planning Committee' had reported to the Secretary of the Navy, Josephus Daniels:[1]

> 'As it seems probable that Great Britain will make every effort to attain the same relative showing in aerial strength as she has in naval strength; the prestige that she would attain by successfully carrying out the first trans-Atlantic flight would be of great assistance to her . . . in view of the fact that the first successful airplane was produced in this country and that the United States developed the first seaplane, it would seem most fitting that the first trans-Atlantic flight should be carried out upon the initiative of the United States Navy.

The Boulton-Paul twin-engined P8, based on the 'Bourges' bomber.
(Real Photo/Ian Allan)

The opportunity, like so many opportunities in Britain between the Wars, was missed. The Establishment could not see it and the Treasury was in one of its most parsimonious moods. So Winston Churchill told the House of Commons in 1920: 'Civil aviation must fly by itself, the Government cannot possibly hold it up in the air'. The industry struggled and panted on until today there is the unattractive spectacle of probably 80 per cent of the free world's civil aircraft, and most of its large airliners, being built in the United States.

[1]No sailor but an ex-journalist and great supporter of the US Navy. It is said, perhaps untruthfully, that on going aboard a battleship for the first time he remarked: 'Good Lord, the durned thing's hollow'.

Kennedy-Sikorsky 'Giant'. (Jane's *Aircraft* 1919)

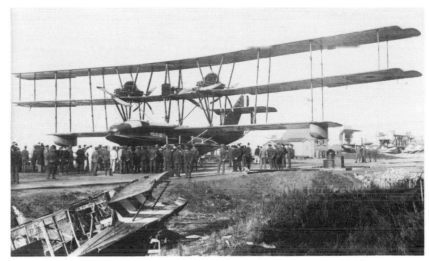

The Felixstowe 'Fury' giant flying-boat.
(Imperial War Museum)

The *Daily Mail* prize attracted eleven entries, all but one British. The American naval team, who were planning with great thoroughness to be first across, had not entered for the prize — giving as a reason 'that it would be ethically improper for them to enter the contest with all resources of the national exchequer behind them'[1] which shows a nicety of feeling that it would be difficult to detect in American thinking on aviation matters since. An alternative reason for their absence was given in *Flight* at the time who wrote that Franklin D. Roosevelt, the Assistant Secretary of the Navy, had said that they could not be a contestant for a prize given by private enterprise. The writer Richard K. Smith perhaps puts it best: 'As a government organisation, the US Navy refused to consider itself or any of its personnel eligible in this competition. There was nevertheless a prize in the transatlantic air race of 1919 that transcended all of the money in the world — and that was the immortal honour of being *first!*"[2]

The possibility of an RAF team consisting of a rigid airship, a Porte flying-boat and a Handley Page bomber was discussed but presumably was killed by the Treasury, as was apparently the sending of the *Felixstowe Fury* until it solved the problem by destroying itself.

[1] *Air Atlantic* by Alan Wykes. Hamish Hamilton, 1967.
[2] *First Across* by Richard K. Smith. Naval Institute, 1973.

Freddie Raynham, one of Britain's best pilots.
(Associated Newspapers)

Indeed, RAF officers were not officially released to take part in the event until February 1919 and altogether, especially compared with the US Navy's massive participation, British Government interest and help was minimal, limited to some meteorological help and precious little else.

Rumours had spoken of a Canadian-built five-engined Handley Page to be piloted by the famous Canadian 'Ace' Lt. Col. R. Collishaw DSO, with O'Brien, Fuller and Robinson as crew and a huge, new British seaplane for the French pilot, René Fonck, was once mentioned. A Caproni triplane with five engines, *White Eagle,* was indeed mentioned in one list of entries but no more was heard of it. Mr Rodman Wanamaker's name crops up again with talk of an entry of a large Curtiss twin-engined flying boat to be piloted by a British pilot — Donald McCulloch. However, eleven entries is impressive enough, even though only five went to the Post.

In alphabetical order they were:

Name & Type	Country	Engine(s)	Type of plane	Pilot & crew
Alliance Seabird	UK	One Napier Lion 450 hp	Land biplane	J. A. Peters & Capt. W. R. Curtis
Boulton & Paul P8	UK	Two Napier Lion 450 hp	Land biplane	Major Savory Capt. Woolner A. L. Howarth
Fairey IIIC (modified)	UK/ Canadian	One Rolls-Royce Eagle 375 hp	Seaplane biplane	S. Pickles & A. G. D. West
Handley Page VI500	UK	Four Rolls-Royce Eagle 365 hp	Land biplane (WWl bomber)	Major Brackley Admiral Mark Kerr Major T. Gran F. Wyatt
Kennedy-Dawson (ex-Sikorsky)	UK	Four Napier Lion 450 hp	Land biplane	
Martinsyde Raymor	UK	One Rolls-Royce Falcon 285 hp	Land biplane	F. Raynham & Capt. Morgan
Short S538 Shirl Shamrock	UK	One Rolls-Royce Eagle 350 hp	Land biplane (WWl torpedo bomber)	Major J. C. P. Wood & Capt. C. C. Wyllie
Sopwith Atlantic	UK	One Rolls-Royce Eagle 350 hp	Land biplane	H. G. Hawker & R. Mackenzie Grieve
Sundstedt Sunrise	US/ Swedish	Two Liberty 400 hp	Seaplane biplane	Capt. Sundstedt & Major Morgan
Vickers Vimy	UK	Two Rolls-Royce Eagle 400 hp	Land biplane (WWl bomber)	J. Alcock & A. Whitten Brown
Whitehead	UK	three or four? Liberty 400 hp	Land biplane	Capt. Payze & two others

Before describing the fortunes of the five aircraft which might be said to have gone to the starting line, namely the Short Shirl *Shamrock,* the Sopwith *Atlantic,* the Martinsyde *Raymor,* the four-engined Handley Page and the Vickers Vimy; it may be of some interest to know what happened to the other entries.

The Alliance *Seabird* was built by a subsidiary of Waring & Gillow, the furniture firm. Photographs show it to be a conventional tractor biplane with a span of 53 ft but with a roomy cabin body with chairs. Clearly designed as a passenger carrier, its cabin allowed the pilot and navigator to be housed 'inside'. Its range was said to be 3000 miles and its speed 140 mph. It did not attempt the crossing but later acquired merit by flying from London to Madrid non-stop.

The Boulton & Paul design looked attractive, a twin-engined biplane with a span of 59 ft; it also had a roomy cabin body, although the pilot was 'outside' in the weather. It was based on the Bourges bomber and had a supposed range of 3850 miles; after two hours in the air it was said to be capable of staying aloft on one engine. The aircraft was designed as a four-seater but the transatlantic version had part of the cabin space fitted with extra tanks. The machine was alleged to have the high top speed of 148 mph. However, the first of the two to be built crashed on its first test flight and the second machine was not ready in time to compete for the prize.

The Fairey entry for the race was first stated in the *Daily Mail* to be a 15-ton flying boat. As this could not be ready in time the entry was switched to one of their standard IIIC types with a Rolls-Royce Eagle VIII engine of 375 hp. However, it appears that this was not a 'slightly modified' IIIC as first stated but a considerably modified aircraft. The Fairey *Atlantic* when put together in Canada differed radically from the standard IIIC, first by having an extra bay added to the wings so that there were three pairs of struts on each side of the fuselage and secondly by the fitting of a single covered-in cockpit, with two seats in echelon; extra tankage was also put into the bottom of the fuselage. The Fairey was interesting also in that it had movable flaps at the trailing edge of the wings to give increased

Raynham's 'Raymor' at take-off.
(Associated Newspapers)

The 'Raymor' crash. (Associated Newspapers)

lift at take-off and alighting. It would seem questionable whether this machine would have had enough speed to compete effectively for the prize.

The Kennedy Aircraft Company of Newcastle-upon-Tyne was reported to be planning a four-seater Kennedy-Dawson biplane for Mr Dawson's entry. Kennedy had been an English aviation pioneer in Russia where he had worked with Sikorsky. He returned to England when war broke out. He designed and had built at the Gramophone Company at Hayes a huge biplane with 142 ft span. However the Air Ministry would only allow him four 200 hp British-built Salmson engines of inadequate power. For the Atlantic attempt something similar was no doubt intended, a modified Sikorsky design with a span of 108 ft and four Napier Lion engines in pairs in tandem, each pair driving a tractor airscrew. This big machine was designed to have an enclosed cabin for four warmed by the engine exhaust and was also to be built at the Gramophone Company at Hayes. It seems doubtful if this plane ever reached the status of an official entry or indeed that it was ever constructed, although it was stated that two would be built, to fly the Atlantic from east to west and from west to east.

The Whitehead machine seems also to have been only on the drawing board though a formal entry was made and Capt. Payze was named as its pilot. In one account, it was described as a 120 ft biplane with one Liberty motor, which sounds wrong; another account that it had four engines is more credible. It was reported that the Whitehead would make the attempt the hard way, starting from Whitehead Park, Feltham, and refuelling at Oranmore, Co. Galway.

The other non-starter was the American/Scandinavian entry, the Sundstedt-Hannevig seaplane built by the Witteman Lewis Aircraft

Co. in Newark, N.J. This was a big aircraft, a biplane with unequal
span, 100 ft on the upper plane and 71½ ft on the lower; with two
Liberty engines driving pusher airscrews it weighed 10,000 lb all up.
Its backer, the Norwegian Christopher Hannevig, had it specially
built for the event with an enclosed cabin for the crew of two but
unfortunately it was wrecked on 27 March on test when in the hands
of the Russian aeronaut Commander Czenzski. Capt. Sundstedt
had told his financial backer not to let anyone other than himself fly
the *Sunrise* but he was ignored and it crashed at the Bayonne Yacht
Club.

The first to take off for the *Daily Mail* prize was the converted
Short Shirl torpedo-bomber, *Shamrock*. This was a good-looking
plane, a wide-span (62 ft) single-engined biplane with one 385 hp
Rolls-Royce Eagle engine; it was a standard Short torpedo-bomber
modified by fitting larger wings with three bays instead of two each
side and mounting a large cylindrical tank between the wheels where
the torpedo was normally carried. Major Wood and Capt. Wyllie
were the crew, sitting in tandem, the former piloting. For some
reason they chose to fly from east to west, intending to fuel at
Bawnmore near Limerick. However, on the way to Ireland on 18
April from Holyhead, the *Shamrock's* engine failed and it made a
forced descent to the sea. The damaged aircraft was towed ashore
and that was the end of the attempt.

The remaining four entries, the Handley Page, the Martinsyde,
the Sopwith and the Vickers, made for Newfoundland and its
favourable winds, eyeing each other and waiting for the weather.

The Sopwith *Atlantic* was a good-looking biplane, based on the
Sopwith B1 bomber developed at the end of the war from the
Cuckoo torpedo bomber. It was a 'special' built for the job, with a
deeper fuselage than the B1 and a wider span of 46½ ft. The
undercarriage could be jettisoned after take-off and so add 7 mph or
more in speed; a small boat formed the top of the fuselage. It had a
good crew; the pilot was Harry Hawker, the popular Australian
flyer and Sopwith's chief test pilot. In spite of having had no fighting

The 'Raymor' in Newfoundland.
(Canadian National Aviation Museum)

service, because of health, he was probably the best-known pilot in England.

Hawker was born in 1889 at Moorabin, Victoria; he became an expert motor mechanic and driver and came over to England early in 1912 with two Australian friends to get into flying. The present generation of relatives believes that Harry Hawker was without doubt descended from the family of the wildly eccentric Cornish poet-parson Robert Hawker of Morwenstow, known to this day as the author of the lines:

> 'And shall Trelawny die?
> Here's twenty thousand Cornish men
> Will know the reason why!'[1]

One of Hawker's friends, Kauper, had got a job with young T. O. M. Sopwith's flying school at Brooklands which had started on 1 February 1912. Hawker worked for Commer cars at 7d. an hour and later for Mercedes at 9½d. Kauper brought Hawker into Sopwith's on 12 July 1912. Sopwith taught Hawker to fly and it was immediately clear that he was a winner. Another pupil of Sopwith's at that time was Hugh 'Boom' Trenchard, the father of the RAF.

Later in 1912 Sopwith progressed from keeping a flying school to building aeroplanes and Hawker, after a triumphal return to Australia, came back to be his chief test pilot. Hawker was an extrovert, hearty personality but not flamboyant or reckless as a pilot; Sir Miles Thomas (later Lord Thomas) described him as 'this bright-eyed human dynamo from Australia'. His navigator for the Atlantic attempt was an experienced, quiet naval officer, called Kenneth Mackenzie Grieve, who had been navigating officer of the seaplane carrier *Campania* during the war. They were complementary in knowledge and opposites in personality.

Hawker eventually died of a heart attack in the air while practising for the Aerial Derby of 1921, but Mackenzie Grieve lived until 1943, dying a natural death in Canada. Hawker's name lives on in the title of the aviation/engineering giant Hawker-Siddeley while the Sopwith name in aviation is just a memory. It was a fascinating experience as recently as March 1978 for me to meet and talk with Sir Thomas Sopwith, at 90 years old, about the old days. He had obtained his British flying certificate as long ago as 1910 and was a number 31 on the list. One of his most memorable remarks was the throwaway line, 'I more or less gave up flying in 1912'. He not only taught Hawker and Trenchard to fly but also founded the aeroplane company which probably contributed most to Britain's victory of 1918. No fewer than 18,000 Sopwith planes were built. This structure was all dismantled at the end of World War I and a small firm, in the name of Hawker this time, was formed by Sopwith, Hawker and two others to start again in the rigours of peace. It prospered hugely, absorbed Gloster, Armstrong-Siddeley and Avro, and until nationalisation in 1977 served the nation nobly.

---

[1] *Song of the Western Men* by Robert Stephen Hawker.

The Sopwith *Atlantic* did a trial run of 900 miles in nine hours or so, was dismantled and shipped from Liverpool to Newfoundland in the SS *Digby* on 18 March, arriving on 29 March 1919. It was considered to have a good chance and to be capable of flying over in 19½ hours.

Raynham's Martinsyde, the *Raymor,* named for him and his navigator Capt. Morgan, was a smaller and lighter biplane than the Sopwith, with a smaller span, 41 ft, and a less powerful engine, a 285 hp Rolls-Royce Falcon. The navigator sat behind the pilot with the advantage of a glazed cabin. Freddy Raynham, chief test pilot for Martinsyde, was the extrovert pilot type like Hawker and like Alcock of the Vimy team; his navigator, who had a wooden leg from the war, was also cheerful and popular. They left Liverpool on 27 March and arrived in St John's on 11 April. Both crews spent a

Crowds round the 'Raymor' before take-off.
(Canadian National Aviation Museum)

frustrating time finding a suitable airfield and waiting for the winter to go away.

Hawker found the passable field at Glendinning's Farm at Mt Pearl about six miles from St John's, and Raynham a field near Quidi Vidi Lake at the suburb of St John's called Pleasantville. Hawker and Raynham agreed to fly together and the long wait for the weather was not made more attractive by the knowledge that a huge four-engined Handley Page V1500 was coming over, with an expected take-off date in May, and that a twin-engined Vickers Vimy was a late entry. Added to this the knowledge that the US Navy team of flying boats, and what was still a secret, reinforced by a C-class blimp airship, was preparing to be first across, must have made the month of April a frustrating time in spite of the comforts of Cochrane's Hotel.

The Handley Page V1500 was a late arrival, though not as late as the Vimy, but its sad story may perhaps be told here to get it out of the way of the main drama. This huge machine with its span of 126 ft and all-up weight of 16 tons, carried a crew of four; Major H. C. Brackley was pilot, Major Trygve Gran was co-pilot and navigator, Admiral Mark Kerr was assistant navigator, one supposes, and F. Wyatt was flight engineer. Brackley was a well-known pilot and later became Air Superintent of Imperial Airways.

Major Gran, the first man to fly the North Sea, was an experienced pilot who was later the last survivor of Scott's last expedition to the Antarctic and one of the party to find Scott's dead body. Admiral Mark Kerr, who had hoped to fly the Atlantic with Hamel in 1914, had been involved in Greek politics when naval attaché in Athens early in World War I; he had later been chief of naval operations in the Adriatic and Vice-Chief of the Air Staff.

The V1500 had been built with the intention of bombing Berlin and returning some of the misery handed out by the Zeppelins and Gothas to London. It was fully capable of flying the Atlantic but assembly and trials at Harbour Grace about 80 miles from St John's were slow, though they did put the wind up the Vimy crew when they flew over their assembly camp at Quidi Vidi.

At any rate, when Hawker and Grieve left on 18 May, the Handley Page was not ready and still not ready when Alcock and Brown left on 14 June. The Atlantic having been flown, the Handley Page camp abandoned the attempt and stood by for orders; on 4 July they took off to fly to New York. They were in wireless touch with the airship R34, which was also New York bound, but they did not see it. With its four-man crew and an extra engineer and an extra rigger, the V1500 took off but developed trouble in two engines and had to put down at Parrsboro, Nova Scotia. By landing on rough ground damage was done to the undercarriage, fuselage and the lower wing. Spare parts were sent out from England but the Handley Page could not leave Parrsboro until 9 October when with 12 aboard — a Canadian record — it at last reached New York.

The next rather forlorn task for this machine was to attempt a run to Chicago for the American Express Company with a cargo of garments, furs and suchlike costly freight. In the cold weather, things froze up and a forced landing was made in Pennsylvania whence the goods went on by train. Finally the bomber took off on 16 November for the last time and the crew, unable to find the aerodrome, landed it on the racecourse at Cleveland, Ohio, where there was insufficient space for its wide wingspan: it was damaged again and a write-off.

What set Hawker and Raynham off on Sunday 18 May in spite of poor though improving weather was the news, false as it turned out, that the American flying boats which had left Trepassey Bay,

Mackenzie Grieve and Harry Hawker.
(Associated Newspapers)

*Harry Hawker's return, on a
police horse.*
(Associated Newspapers)

Newfoundland, on 16 May had reached the Azores. Realising that
they could still be away and over before the Americans could make
it, Hawker and Grieve rushed off to the field to get airborne.
According to Bob Dicker, Alcock and Brown's chief mechanic who
had just arrived in Newfoundland, Raynham, who was walking with
him as Hawker roared overhead, said: 'The bugger's double-crossed
me; we were to have gone together'.[1] This statement had the ring of
truth but it must be said that other accounts say that Hawker did at
least let Raynham know that he was off. The *New York Times*
reported his message as: 'How about old Tinsides? Tell Raynham
I'll greet him at Brooklands, England'. The *New York Times* also
reports that Raynham had called on Hawker that morning and
found him looking at a possible storm-free route south of the Great
Circle at which Freddy said: 'No good, old top; I've been trying all
morning to work out that course; it won't do, it's too far'. Raynham
and Morgan then rushed out to their machine and made an
attempted take-off an hour after Hawker had left. Their runway at
Quidi Vidi was inadequate, less suitable than Hawker's at
Glendinning's Field, a stiff crosswind was blowing, and they had
just lifted off[2] when a side gust hit them and they crashed heavily,
luckily without catching fire. Raynham was unhurt, but Morgan
received cuts to his head and eye and had to return to England. To
complete the Raynham story, the Martinsyde was repaired and
Raynham had another try on 17 July with a new navigator, either
Lt. Biddlecombe or Lt. Ford; accounts differ. Again the aircraft
crashed at take-off and that was the end of it.

[1]See *Transport Pioneers of the 20th Century* — The Transport Trust. Patrick Stephens 1981.
[2]The later accounts mention three attempts at take-off but the contemporary account by the
New York Times correspondent does not say so. My conclusion is that there was only one.

Hawker and Grieve leaving their rescue ship. (Associated Newspapers)

Hawker and Grieve had hoped to leave with the April full moon in mid-month but the weather had been uniformly bad and was still poor when they left after their six weeks' work and Raynham and Morgan crashed. But for the news that US flying boats had reached the Azores on 17 May — in fact only one had — they would probably have waited again.

The take-off was difficult — they all were — and Hawker had to deal with a crosswind and an L-shaped runway. Once out to sea, Hawker jettisoned the undercarriage which was later picked up and is now in the St. John's museum.

The flight went smoothly and normally for several hours at 105 mph, normally that is in that the wireless almost immediately gave up the ghost, while the engine went serenely on; then as night fell rough air, cloud, fog and rain gripped the machine. About 11 p.m. GMT after just over five hours' flying Hawker noticed that the water temperature was higher than it should have been and did not respond when he opened the radiator shutters; indeed it continued to rise. Hawker suspected that accumulated rust and extraneous solids were blocking the filter in the circulation system and felt he might clear it by stopping the engine and diving, so they went down from 12,000 to 9000 ft and started up again; this worked for a time but by 12.30 a.m. GMT when they were about 800 miles out the temperature was up again. They repeated the diving manoeuvre twice again but it did not work and their radiator began to boil. Although comfortable enough in their special flying suits they continued uneasily at 12,000 ft in better weather, guided by the moon and stars, but by morning another huge and insurmountable cloud bank confronted them. They could not buffet through this so Hawker decided to come down to 1000 ft where the air was clear. After this descent with the engine off, there was an instant when disaster was upon them as the engine would not restart; only after furious pumping could Grieve get the pressure tank to deliver petrol and let the engine restart, only a few feet above the waves.

That morning, about 1000 miles away from Newfoundland and over halfway across when they had come down below the cloud base, Hawker and Grieve found they were 150 miles south of their course and close to the eastbound shipping lane. With the engine rapidly boiling away the last of its water, Ireland was out of the question so Hawker and Grieve began to look for a ship amid the squalls and deteriorating weather. About 7.00 a.m. GMT with a shout of joy they sighted the small Danish tramp *Mary* (Capt. Duhn) homeward bound from Norfolk, Virginia, to Aarhus and after alerting her with Verey lights put the *Atlantic* down in her path. They were able to detach and launch their small boat; the Danes put a boat out and Hawker and Grieve, still relatively warm and dry in their special life-saving suits, were picked up. With the heavy seas

Imaginative sketch – down in the Atlantic, 1919. (Flight)

running they were not able to salvage anything, but the Sopwith remained afloat and the wreck was picked up by the American freighter *Lake Charlotteville* with the bag of mail on 23 May and was later exhibited on the roof of Selfridge's store in London.

Hawker and Mackenzie Grieve were rescued at 8.30 a.m. GMT on 19 May rather over fourteen and a half hours and 1050 miles after leaving Newfoundland.

To the outside world they had just disappeared into the blue for their rescuer had no wireless and they saw no other ship to relay the news of their survival. With every day anxiety mounted and hope faded and the announcement of the finding of the wreck of their plane added to the certainty that they must be dead. The King sent messages of condolence and the *Daily Mail* undertook to provide for Hawker's widow and Mackenzie Grieve's next of kin with £10,000, the amount of the prize money, though the sum still stood for the first successful flight. Mrs Hawker, however, remained serenely certain of their survival.

Then on Sunday 25 May, a week after they had left Newfoundland, the incredible happened. The coast guard station on the Butt of Lewis received a signal from a small Danish ship which said: 'Saved hands, Sopwith aeroplane' to which the question 'Is it Hawker? was answered 'Yes'. The destroyer *Woolston* came up to the *Mary* and took the aviators off and to Scapa Flow where they slept in the flagship HMS *Revenge*. From there all the way to London by train they were given a conquering hero's welcome: huge crowds, cheers, speeches and in London dense numbers and a Rolls-Royce cavalcade. So thick was the crowd that Hawker could only progress on a policemen's horse. Britain gave way to the delirious adulation which is reserved for spectacular or unparalleled failure, for a return from death and for the redemption of hope deferred. The King gave the flyers the Air Force Cross and the *Daily Mail* a consolation prize of £5000.

The Sopwith "Atlantic" of Hawker and Grieve. (Flight)

4.
First Across

The United States Navy was determined to be the first across, come what may, and mounted a huge exercise to achieve it. Mustered for the crossing were a division of the latest flying boats, four of them, a non-rigid airship of the newest type and in support no less than 53[1] destroyers strung out at 50-mile intervals from Cape Cod to the Bay of Biscay via Newfoundland, the Azores, and Lisbon. These were backed up by five battleships, two old cruisers and several auxiliaries to a total of 66 warships. And yet the grim Atlantic, 'that old grey widow-maker', nearly beat them all.

One of the flying boats was a non-starter; two came down at sea, of which one sank and the other limped into port in the Azores. As for the blimp, it was torn from its moorings in Newfoundland and blown out to sea, a total loss. One flying boat, the NC4, made it and made history, but it took its time. As for the warships they were a splendid aid in fair weather but in foul they might just as well not have been there for the radio communications on two out of the three flying boats failed and, when it mattered, connections were conspicuous by their rarity. Only the NC4 had superior radio equipment and used it properly, which was the principal reason for its success.

Flying boat development had been going on on both sides of the Atlantic during World War I stemming largely from the designs of Glenn Curtiss. He himself continued on from the 1914 *America* and John Porte in Felixstowe developed his series of F-boats from the same original machine. The trend was towards bigger flying-boats with longer range to combat the German U-boats in mid-Atlantic and the Americans at any rate imagined flying boats capable of crossing the Atlantic to reach the theatre of war. There was close colaboration between the naval air services of both countries and for a time, from 1914 to 1916, Lieutenant Commander Towers, a pioneer of US naval aviation, was an Extra Naval Attaché in London.

So in September 1917 Admiral Taylor, head of the US Navy's Construction Corps, got together his leading constructors in the

[1]Eight between Montauk, L.I., and Newfoundland, 22 between Newfoundland and the Azores, 13 between the Azores and Lisbon and 10 between Lisbon and Ushant.

Flying boat NC-4 in flight.
(Science Museum)

aviation branch, Hunsaker, Richardson and Westervelt, to specify a really big flying boat. They then called in Glenn Curtiss to build it.

Curtiss submitted two alternative plans, one for a three-engined biplane and the other with no less than five engines. The smaller machine was chosen. The design differed from that of other flying-boats of the day in having a short body like a sabot and the tail assembly mounted on three booms, two springing from the upper wing and one from the tail of the boat body. The wings were of unequal size and separated, clear of the engine nacelles by three pairs of struts on each side. Large vertical stabilisers were attached to the extremities of the upper wing. The tail assembly was high enough to be well clear of the water and consisted of three rudders between twin elevators.

After much coming and going over what was an unorthodox design and consultations with Commander Porte a final design was drawn up by Richardson by December 1917 and orders were given by the Navy Department for four of these NC — Navy Curtiss — flying-boats, to be built at Garden City, Long Island, near their expected naval station at Rockaway Beach, close to the present Kennedy Airport at Idlewild.

The British Aviation Commission in July 1918 inspected NC-1 and did not think much of it; and it must be added that tank tests on models a month later upset Richardson into believing that it could not be got off the water with a full load. However, by 4 October 1918, NC-1 was ready for its first trial flight; it performed well and Richardson's design looked good, although the aircraft was afterwards considerably modified and the later ones differed from the prototype.

In NC-1's original form the power plant consisted of three 12-cylinder Liberty engines of a nominal 400 hp driving four-bladed tractor airscrews. This engine, essentially a Packard Motors' design, was perhaps the United States' biggest contribution to aviation in World War I. The two pilots sat side-by-side in the centre nacelle immediately behind one engine and so were buffeted by a perpetual gale from its propeller.

NC-1 turned out to be under-powered although on 27 November 1918 it flew with no fewer than fifty men on board plus one stowaway — the first in aerial history. It was calculated that a fourth engine would add 1600 lb in weight but gain 3200 lb in load carried. So NC-2, which was originally built with three engines (the centre one a pusher), was rebuilt with four Liberty motors in two pairs in tandem leaving the centre nacelle for the sole occupation of the pilots. In this form she became the NC-2T. This extra power gave better performance but an alternative arrangement of four engines in a one-two-one pattern promised less disturbance from the propellers' wash and this was adopted for NC-3 and NC-4; later NC-1 was altered to this style. This change had the advantage of housing the pilots within the hull with the rest of the crew. The wings

Welcoming British aircraft at Plymouth. (BBC/Hulton)

of the flying boats were dark yellow in colour[1] and the hull and floats painted grey-blue. The US roundels of the time — white, blue, red from the centre[2] — were on the wings and red, white and blue vertical stripes on the rudders.

Meanwhile, with the war over and these 'Nancy' (NC) boats under construction, there was some rivalry over who was to be the first officer to be selected to fly the Atlantic. On 9 July 1918 Lt.

[1] The models on display in the Smithsonian Air & Space Museum in Washington show grey wings which is probably incorrect, as pieces of the original wing fabric on sale there are dark yellowish-brown in colour.
[2] The British markings were of course red, white, blue from the centre and the French blue, white and red.

Richard E. Byrd, later famous for his polar expeditions, requested that he be assigned to fly the Atlantic when NC-1 was built. Instead he was sent to Canada to find a suitable location on the coast of Newfoundland for handling and maintenance of large seaplanes and Trepassey Bay, about eighty miles south-west of St. John's, was selected. This assignment proved Byrd's undoing as an order was issued from Washington at the end of the war which said: 'No officer or man who has had foreign duty will be permitted to be a member of the transatlantic flight expedition. This includes those who have been on Canadian detail'. So Commander Towers who had been in on the planning from the start and who had also applied for the job of commanding the flight got it and also a command without precedent in the US Navy, being appointed formally in command of 'NC Seaplane Division One' which gave him the status approximately equal to that of a commander of a destroyer flotilla. The officers and men were assigned to the three surviving flying-boats NC-1, NC-3 and NC-4 after NC-2 had been broken up and cannibalised and NC-3 became the flagship. There was no place for the unhappy Byrd who was allowed to go as far as Newfoundland as a passenger in NC-3; then he was reprieved and told he would be allowed to join the crew of the airship C5 which was to be part of the expedition. NC-1 also had a passenger to Trepassey Bay, Ensign C. J. McCarthy, who had worked out the best four-engined configuration for the flying-boats.

The run-up period to the attempt was far from trouble-free, although agreements with the British, Newfoundland, Canadian and Portuguese Governments were smoothly arranged and there was a good air of international co-operation. NC-1 was badly damaged in a storm late in March 1919 and that put an end to hopes for a four-plane flight as NC-2, which had been kept for experiments, was finally used to supply parts for repairing NC-1 which was also being rebuilt to the four-engine layout of NC-3 and 4. The last two boats were delivered late: NC-3 first flew on 23 April and NC-4 was completed only on 1 May so that the first selected date of departure, 5 May had to be changed. So while NC-3 was ready and fit, NC-1 and NC-4 were still being worked on when in the

NC-1 flying-boat, as built.
(Imperial War Museum)

early hours of 5 May the whole enterprise seemed lost for fire broke out in the NC hangar during fuelling. The tail of NC-4 was damaged and one wing of NC-1. It looked a bad prospect but by superhuman efforts, using wing and tail sections of NC-2, all the damage was made good by midnight of that day. More troubles followed; on 7 May a small seaplane crashed into a gasholder at the base, killing both pilots, while Machinist's Mate Howard lost a hand in the arc of one of NC-4's propellers and so his place in its crew. On 7 May Towers told the press that because of continued foul weather the flight was indefinitely postponed; then next morning, 8 May, with a better meteorological report, suddenly and surprisingly they were off.

The successful NC-4 at Plymouth.
(BBC/Hulton)

What were they like, these Navy flying-boats which were about to astonish the world? First of all they were *big*, very big and, with the departure of the *Felixstowe Fury*, the biggest flying boats in the world. The upper wing had a span of 126 ft and the lower of 96 ft; the upper panel of the tail assembly had a span of 37 ft 11 in., bigger than a fighter's. Their overall length was 68 ft 2 in., of which the hull accounted for 44 ft 9 in. The weight, fully loaded, was 28,000 lb, with a crew of six.

The officer in command of each flying boat was the navigator, who was stationed right up in the bow; when required to make an observation or work the flares mounted forward he had to stand up and take his sight or observe the drift in the full gale of 80 mph. Down in the navigator's cockpit was an upholstered box to sit on, instruments, a chart table, charts and log books. One of Byrd's invaluable new bubble sextants was in the equipment. Behind the navigator was a space to lie down, then the pilot's cockpit, a two-seater open to the air with bench seat. Further aft, behind the fuel tanks, came the after cockpit for the engineers and below them the radio apparatus and the radio operator. There was no heating and no parachutes were carried, the engineers being fitted with belts with life-lines for working on the engines in flight. One passenger remarked on the bleakness of flying in these boats, thus:

'I was privileged to be an observing passenger aboard the NC-1 on an eight hour non-stop proving flight. I thought it would never end. Its cruising speed was slow, 80-85 mph, and there was no shelter for a 'super cargo' like me, and it was cold and windy almost beyond endurance for so long a time. No lunch either[1]'.

The crews named for the transatlantic attempt were:—

NC-1

Lt. Cmdr. P. N. L. Bellinger	*Commander*
Lt. Cmdr. M. A. Mitscher	*Pilot*
Lt. L. T. Barrin	*Pilot*
Lt. H. Sadenwater	*Radio*
Ch. Machs. Mate R. Christensen	*Engineer*
Ch. Machs. Mate C. I. Kessler	*Engineer*

NC-3 (Flagship of the Division)

Cmdr. J. H. Towers	*Commander*
Cmdr. H. C. Richardson	*Pilot*
Lt. D. H. McCulloch	*Pilot*
Lt. Cmdr. R. A. Lavender	*Radio*
Lt. B. Rhodes	*Engineer*
Ch. Boatswain L. R. Moore	*Engineer*

(Lt. B. Rhodes was off-loaded at Newfoundland and did not fly on).

NC-4

Lt. Cmdr. A. C. Read	*Commander*
Lt. (Coast Guard) E. F. Stone	*Pilot*
Lt. W. Hinton	*Pilot*
Lt. J. L. Breese	*Engineer*
Ensign H. C. Rodd	*Radio*
Ch. Machs. Mate E. S .Rhoads*	*Engineer*

*In place of Machs. Mate E. C. Howard who was incapacitated.

Airship C-5

Lt. Cmdr. E. W. Coil
Lt. J. B. Lawrence
Lt. M. H. Esterly
Ensign D. P. Campbell
Ch. Machs. Mate H. S. Blackburn
Ch. Machs. Mate T. L. Moorman

[1]Grover Loening in *Take Off into Greatness.* Putnam, 1968.

NC-2 flying boat with 4 engines in pairs.
(Flight)

After the take-off from Rockaway on 8 May NC-1 (Bellinger) and NC-3 (Towers) in spite of some rough weather reached Halifax, Nova Scotia, that evening but NC-4 (Read) was in serious trouble. Passing Cape Cod the centre pusher engine had had to be stopped because of low oil pressure. Soon afterwards the centre tractor engine slung a connecting rod through the crank-case so Read ordered the flying-boat to alight. Wireless communications which had signalled their distress now failed, so eighty miles from land the NC-4 could do nothing but taxi slowly towards Chatham,

NC-1 flying-boat in original state with 3 engines. (Flight)

Massachusetts, with the two remaining engines. At one time one of these failed but the mechanics got it going again and dawn 9 May found Read and his crew off Chatham. The ruined engine was replaced and the others repaired but NC-4, the 'lame duck', which was ready to leave Chatham on 11 May was confined there by storms until the 13th.

Meanwhile NC-1 and NC-3, after renewing their propellers at Halifax, set off for their base at Trepassey Bay, Newfoundland, on

10 May, arriving alongside their mother ship USS *Aroostook* that evening. There they too were weather-bound.

On the 13th NC-4's troubles continued as one of the engine starters broke and after a rush to get a spare flown from Rockaway, she took off on the morning of 14 May with vibration in the new engine and dirt in the fuel line, but reached Halifax that evening. Next morning NC-4 left Halifax but had to put back to clean the carburettors, only leaving around noon on the 15th. From then on Read and his crew made good time, meeting on the way the gasbag of the airship C-5 which had blown away from its moorings just before. When the NC-4 reached Trepassey Bay at dusk on the 15th Read was dismayed to see NC-1 and NC-3 manoeuvring to take off. Towers had been willing to leave without NC-4 but bad weather had held up the two sound flying boats; after trying all the afternoon of May 15 to get airborne, they called it a day. So the team was reunited, NC-4 was fitted with a new engine and three propellers overnight and next day, 16 May, all three aircraft were ready. Towers failed to get off again on his first attempt on the 16th and so decided to lighten his flying-boat by dumping some of his equipment and leaving one of his engineers, Rhodes, behind. Then, about 6 p.m. local time (22.00 GMT) they were ready to leave in concert and this time they all took off. But then, however, NC-4 was no longer the 'lame duck' but the fittest and liveliest of the three.

The sad story of the dirigible C-5 comes in here. This was one of the Navy's latest type of non-rigid airship, built for coastal patrol and anti-submarine work, like the British and French blimps which had done good service in the war. C-5 was 192 ft long and had a volume of 182,000 cu. ft; it carried a crew of six and was powered by

NC-4 arriving at Lisbon. (Science Museum)

The US Secretary of the Navy, Josephus Daniels and Assistant Secretary, Franklin D. Roosevelt with the US flying-boat crews.
(Smithsonian Institution)

two Union 120 hp engines. Not much publicity was attached to the C-5 but in fact she made a notable non-stop flight from Montauk on Long Island to Quidi Vidi field near St John's, Newfoundland. C-5 was commanded by Cmdr. E. W. Coil and was to be joined by Lt. Richard Byrd who had had a lift up to Newfoundland in the NC-3. Byrd presumably was intended to replace one of the others.

C-5 had left Montauk on 14 May and after a splendid flight of nearly 1200 nautical miles in 25 hours and 50 minutes had managed despite rough weather, extreme cold and confusing radio signals to find a recognisable spot at Topsail on Newfoundland whence she had followed the railway to St John's. She 'docked' at Quidi Vidi field in time for a late breakfast for her crew. Then in the afternoon of 15 May, while a ground crew under Lt. Charles G. Little was working on the airship, a fierce squall blew up, gusting to 60 knots, and she tore away from her moorings. The engines could not be started and attempts to rip the envelope failed. Little and the other two men on board had to jump for their lives and the airship blew out to sea unmanned. Chief Machinist's Mate Crampton is reported to have saved the ship's log. A local boy in the crowd of helpers was said to have been killed by one of the mooring ropes, though later accounts stated that he survived. It was certainly a sad day.

Lt. Cmdr. Coil was assuredly an unlucky man. While he was in hospital at the end of 1918 recovering from pneumonia, he received news that his mother and wife had both died, presumably in the post-war influenza epidemic. Then he lost his airship in Newfoundland and finally he lost his life in the wreck of the airship R38 over the Humber in 1921, as did Lt. C. G. Little.

The night that the C-5 was lost, 15 May 1919, there was a maximum gathering of aeronauts in Newfoundland. There were three crews of six in each of the 'Nancies', though one of them was

The damaged NC-3 at the Azores
(Smithsonian Institution)

left behind next day, there was the crew of six from the C-5 plus the now wingless Byrd. The British numbered ten; four with the Handley Page, together with Hawker and Grieve, Raynham and Morgan, and Alcock and Brown newly arrived but without their aircraft. The Americans looked strangely unsailorlike in their dark green Edwardian uniforms, breeches and leather leggings, high tunic collars and small round kepis; they looked somehow like policemen or Italian cavalry.

Although they had taken off on 16 May as a team the three flying boats could not keep together once they were on their way. NC-4 was faster than the others and flew badly if held in check while NC-1 was hard to fly with one of the cannibalised NC-2's wings incorrectly rigged and out of balance. Using the ships strung out along their path Read and the NC-4 made good progress but by dawn the weather thickened and deteriorated. However, Read's radio and his radio officer, Lt. Rodd, were of decisive quality so his navigation was good and although he lost his guiding destroyers in the murk he saw land below in the morning light where he expected to find it and was indeed over Flores, the westernmost island of the Azores, only 250 miles from Ponta Delgada, their destination. But with bad weather coming up again they were content to put down at Horta in the Island of Fayal at 13.23 GMT, 15 hours and 13 minutes after being airborne at Trepassey. The Azores chain, which stretches for nearly 400 miles east to west, worried all the navigators who, in the fog and cloud which they were now meeting, were especially wary of Pico, an island which springs up to 7600 ft straight out of the sea.

While NC-4 was safe and sound in harbour at Horta alongside the old US cruiser *Columbia,* NC-1 and NC-3 were be no means so well off, indeed not well off at all. Their radio direction finding and range were inferior; they were lost.

NC-1 had been hard to handle and with the dawn and all-pervasive cloud and fog Bellinger, realising he was lost and not relishing contact with Pico, decided to come down on the water and take stock. This was a mistake, for a much rougher sea was running than appeared from the air.

At 8.10 a.m. local time (13.10 GMT) on 17 May NC-1 ditched 200 miles north-west of Fayal and was fatally damaged soon after impact, part of the tail being carried away. For five hours NC-1's crew, cold, wet and seasick, bailed for dear life while the pilots tried to keep the engines running to hold the head into the wind and power the radio.

At last the Greek freighter *Ionia* (Capt. Panas) appeared and tried to take the aircraft in tow, but the rough seas prevented it so the airmen abandoned ship and were taken aboard and deposited in Horta with the USS *Columbia*.

Another view of the damaged NC-3. (Smithsonian Institution)

Towers in NC-3 had much the same experience. Realising he was lost he put his ship down within 20 minutes of Bellinger and about 45 miles west of Flores to investigate. Too late he realised that a heavy swell was running and NC-3 was at once damaged by the waves which split the hull and broke the controls. That night in a storm the float on the port wing was also carried away. However, the ship was afloat and the engines were workable in emergencies, so Read set about floating to his destination. Although Pico was sighted about 40 miles off at dawn Towers decided to drift on if possible to Ponta Delgada on the island of São Miguel. So all the rest of that day, 17 May, and for the whole of the 18th, Towers and his crew bailed the water out of their ship and edged the NC-3 along to the east until on the morning of the 19th they were sighted by a US Marine gun post on São Miguel, west of Ponta Delgada. The destroyer *Harding* rushed up to help but Towers, having conserved his fuel and his engines for this last moment, hauled in his distress signal, the US flag upside-down, raised the Stars and Stripes in its correct posture and called: 'Stand off! We're going in under our own power', which they did, having spent over two days on the bosom of the ocean, for the last 24 hours of which the crew had taken turns to lie on the starboard wing to keep the damaged port-side wing out of the water. The crew subsisted on sea-soaked sandwiches and radiator water and, one would add, a pretty proud spirit. The NC-3 arrived at Ponta Delgada at 18.30 GMT on 19 May having flown 1240 miles in 15½ hours and covered 205 miles on the sea in 53 hours. So she arrived at the Azores base ahead of NC-4, but was unfit to continue and had to be taken back to the United States for repairs. Towers was expressly forbidden by the Secretary of the Navy to transfer his 'flag' to the NC-4 or even travel in it as a passenger although such a move would have been in keeping with naval traditions.

Read had apparently been expecting that Towers would resume command and Towers without doubt was bitterly disappointed by the Secretary's ruling. But Josephus Daniels had not been a newspaper man for nothing; he sensed that the public was already acclaiming Read as the hero who conquered the Atlantic and to have deprived him of the honour of leading the completed flight and reaching Europe would have looked like a piece of stuffy Navy organisation, which would have harmed his beloved Navy's reputation and hampered recruiting.

While both men denied any personal estrangement or indeed any feelings in the matter in spite of what the press said, there is no doubt that the memory of Josephus Daniels's decision was never forgotten by either of the men even when they both became Admirals. A correspondent, Bayard Sharp, who served in the US Naval Air Service under Read in World War II, said: 'By then the feelings had cooled down to a sort of Bob Hope — Bing Crosby relationship'. Sharp illustrated this by one incident. When he was undergoing training at Pensacola under Admiral Read there were many different types of men under instruction to learn to fly in the strict Navy way — inexperienced, young, experienced and old. Inevitably there were some anomalies with young instructors trying to teach their grandmothers to suck eggs, in the persons of experienced bush pilots and other mature flyers with hundreds of hours behind them. One of these, a tall Texan, bet his friends 100 dollars that he would make his innocent green instructor bail out. Getting into a near stall upside-down, during aerobatic instruction, or some such near disaster, the Texan grabbed the shock-cords attached to the back of the instructor's metal seat in front of him, pulled back and let go causing a frightful noise and vibration. Then he yelled above the noise: 'She's cracking up!'. The instructor decamped and the Texan came down in the plane to face a court martial. After the court had

Lt. Commander A. C. Read with the Prince of Wales.
(Associated Newspapers)

Engines of the flying-boat NC-4
(Canadian National Aviation Museum)

delivered a severe reprimand and apologies had been offered all round, the little Admiral was later seen talking to the tall Texan. 'How did you do it?' he asked, looking upwards. The Texan explained and added that the mess he had deliberately got into was confusing enough but the noise of the cords beating on the instructor's seat was really awful. 'Ah', said Read, 'thank you very much, I must try it on Towers'.

After a stop in Horta for weather while their British rivals Hawker and Raynham came to grief, Read left for Ponta Delgada on 20 May and in just over an hour and a half reached base. Here, the British pressure being off, they spent nearly a week, leaving for Lisbon and completion of the passage of the Atlantic on 27 May, arriving at dusk (20.01 GMT) on that day after flying all but $9\frac{3}{4}$ hours. Here a great welcome met them and this was repeated when they reached Plymouth on 31 May for a patrol of three British F2a flying boats bearing huge flags of the two nations greeted them; appropriately enough they were Porte flying-boats. The last leg from Lisbon involved stops near Figueira da Foz on the Mondego River in Portugal and at El Ferrol in northern Spain. In all the first passage of the Atlantic took 53 hours and 58 minutes of flying time spread over 23 days and covering 4096 nautical miles. From Newfoundland to Lisbon the NC-4 took 26 hours 41 minutes spread over 11 days.

In all, the American flyers were very well received in Britain and were entertained by the Prince of Wales, Winston Churchill and other Members of Parliament. At a luncheon in their honour at the House of Commons, Major General Seely, Under Secretary of State for Air, said: 'There is no trace of envy on our part. We recognise to the full that you have brilliantly succeeded where we gloriously failed'. Read in his reply said: 'The British people are good winners but they are wonderful losers'. Alas, too true. *Flight* wrote, rather captiously perhaps:

'The Atlantic has at last been crossed in the air and another milestone added to the road of aeronautical progress. By his arrival at Plymouth on Saturday last, Lieut. Commander Read and his machine have created a new record to stand for all time. We have not the slightest desire to belittle what is undoubtedly a very fine performance, but we should not be doing our duty to the future if we refrained from pointing out that, stripped of the glamour of being the first time an aircraft had crossed the Atlantic, the circumstances of the flight are such as to make it rather less wonderful than the simple record would be. As a matter of fact the flight has nothing much of the spectacular about it — it was rather a triumph of organisation than anything else, and it is to the American Naval authorities no less than to Commander Read and the crew of NC-4 that the success of the cross-Atlantic flight is due. For weeks the whole route has been patrolled and marked out by ships of the US Navy, each acting as a kind of mark-boat for the adventure and as

The ill-fated airship C-5 in Newfoundland. (Vickers)

The airship C-5 in Newfoundland.
(Smithsonian Institution)

possible saviour of the crews of the seaplanes in the event of mishap. Nothing has been neglected that could make the success of the flight a matter of almost mathematical certainty, and it has succeeded almost as a matter of course. At the same time, Commander Read and his crew are certainly to be very greatly congratulated upon the successful issue of an enterprise which they were actually the first to essay, and it will be their names which will be handed down to history as being those of the first men to cross the Atlantic in the air.

Harry Hawker was not too gracious: 'still smarting at having been beaten by the unsporting aeronautical steam-roller created by the U.S. Navy'. He ridiculed the NC flight in public as like 'walking down Broadway'. Later he swallowed his sourness and certainly Lord Northcliffe was appreciative.

C. G. Grey in *The Aeroplane* was rather more generous than *Flight* had been:

'All who are concerned with aeronautics in any form or phase must congratulate the American nation on the fact that American aviators have defeated the Atlantic Ocean. Naturally we of the British Empire would have preferred that a British aviator should have been the first to succeed in crossing from the New World to the Old by air, but if it could not be one of ourselves we are glad that the honour should belong to those of British race (Oh dear!).

Also there is pure poetic justice in the victory being won by the Americans. After all, the first people to fly were the Wright brothers in 1903, on a machine of their own build with an engine of their own make. The first flights off and onto water were made by Glenn Curtiss in 1911, also on a machine and engine of his own production. And the first flying-boat was designed and built by Glenn Curtiss in 1913, again with a home-made engine. Who therefore has a better right to be first across the Atlantic than an American crew on an American flying-boat with American engines? We may regret our own failure, but we cannot begrudge America her brilliant success. . . .

The American victory was the deserved result of great personal gallantry, great skill in the design, preparation, care and handling of the machine and her engines, and great ability in seamanship and airmanship. But above all it was a triumph of organisation — which is just where we in this country fail so constantly'.

Pursuing their careers in the Navy, Bellinger, Byrd (who achieved his wish to fly the Atlantic in 1927), Mitscher, Read and Towers all became Admirals. Mitscher became famous as Commander of Task Force 58 in the war against Japan and Byrd for his Polar flights and exploration. Rear Admiral Read became Commander, Fleet Air Norfolk, in World War II and Towers ended as Commander of Task Force 58 in the Pacific Fleet just as the war was won. Glenn Curtiss left aviation and turned to real estate in Florida with success.

Richard K. Smith sums it all up so well in saying that while the world marvelled at the daring, seemingly devil-may-care exploits of Hawker and Grieve, Alcock and Brown, and Lindbergh, it was the meticulous, professional, unexciting, take-no-risks methods of the NC project which really laid the proper foundations of regular, safe and reliable air travel.[1] Invaluable detail is also to be found in the US *Naval Aviation News.*[2]

[1]Richard K. Smith, *First Across,* Naval Institute Press, 1973.
[2]Ted Wilbur's article *The First Flight Across the Atlantic,* Naval Aviation News, May 1969. Smithsonian Institute.

5.
Alcock and Brown

The famous flight of Alcock and Brown sixty-five years ago has been so frequently described that to add one more account may seem superfluous — especially as it is obvious, when one reads the dozen or so narratives already published, that there is only one source of information and that is what these men wrote themselves immediately after it.[1] However, a recent publication of the Transport Trust[2] contains an interview with the late Mr R. E. Dicker who was the sole survivor of the ground crew of the Vickers Vimy team in Newfoundland which may give a fresh impression of the famous event.

The Vickers FB27, the Vimy twin-engined bomber, was designed by the Vickers aviation team under J. K. Pierson. It first flew in November 1917. Like the earlier Handley Page 0/400, it was designed and built quickly to meet the sudden need for heavy bombers on the Allied side. The Vimy, which was no beauty, had a chunky serviceable air and for its duties was of limited weight and size. A compact biplane, its wing span was only 68 ft and its total all-up weight 12,500 lb. The Vimy was built with various engines but for the *Atlantic* machine two 360 hp Rolls-Royce Eagle VIII 12-cylinder engines were used. Normally it carried a crew of three. The Vimy did not see active service in World War I but apart from its numerous long-distance flights it was in RAF service until 1929.

As soon as the problem of a suitable pilot was solved in March 1919 by the choice of John Alcock, Vickers went ahead with a modified Vimy for the transatlantic crossing. The bomb racks were removed, extra tanks fitted in the fuselage and a special fairing was made over the top of one of the fuselage tanks to form an inverted boat which could be detached in an emergency. The front bomber's cockpit was omitted from the nose and also the rear cockpit behind the wings, leaving only a two-seater compartment for the pilot and his one companion. With the extra petrol carried the *Atlantic* Vimy weighed in at 13,500 lb, only about half the weight of the American NC flying boats.

A front wheel was fitted in place of the normal skid but this was

[1] *Our Transatlantic Flight,* Alcock and Brown. Wm. Kimber, 1969.
[2] *Transport Pioneers of the 20th Century.* Patrick Stephens, 1981.

The Vickers 'Vimy' in flight, Newfoundland. (Vickers)

discarded in Newfoundland. All these modifications took about a month and on 18 April 1919, Good Friday, the Vimy did its one and only test flight in England from Brooklands Aerodrome where it had been built.

The aircraft was dismantled, crated and put aboard SS *Glendevon* which sailed on 13 May and reached St. John's, Newfoundland, on 26 May. To have the Vimy ready for test by 9 June was no mean feat. The advance party with Alcock the pilot and Whitten Brown the navigator had left Liverpool on 4 May in the *Mauretania* for Halifax, Nova Scotia, and from there had arrived in St. John's by rail and boat on 13 May.

John Alcock was a Mancunian born in 1892, short, stocky, easy-going and an extrovert. His brother writes that he had a 'cheerful ruddy face, tousled hair and a ready wit delivered with a Lancashire accent'. Among his accomplishments was skill in making treacle toffee and parkin.

He became interested in flying and in 1910 went from his apprenticeship in Manchester to Brooklands to work as mechanic to one of the French pioneers, Maurice Ducrocq with his Maurice Farman biplane. Before he was twenty Alcock had obtained his Royal Aero Club certificate and was an experienced pilot with competition experience when World War I broke out. He joined the

The Vickers 'Vimy' in flight, Newfoundland. (Vickers)

Royal Naval Air Service and was posted as an instructor to Eastchurch where one of his pupils was Flt. Sub. Lt. Warneford who won the VC for shooting down the first Zeppelin.

In 1917 Alcock was posted to Mudros in the eastern Mediterranean where he piloted Handley Page 0/400 twin-engined bombers in sorties against the Turks, including the first raid on Constantinople. He was credited with shooting down seven enemy aircraft and was decorated with the Distinguished Service Cross.

However, in the autumn of 1917 engine failure over enemy territory brought him down; he was captured and suffered a bad month in a disgusting Turkish jail. Eventually, possibly by the intervention of German officers including the Kaiser himself, Alcock and his companions were transferred to an officers' camp in Anatolia where he spent a not unhappy thirteen months as a captive. On demobilisation he went straight to Vickers and on 11

The Vickers 'Vimy' in Newfoundland. (Vickers)

Alcock and Brown in flying kit.
(Vickers)

March 1919 was engaged to fly their modified Vimy for the *Daily Mail* prize.

Arthur Whitten Brown was quite a different type from Alcock, quiet, introspective, studious, an only child. He was an American, born in 1886 in Glasgow when his parents were on a visit. His family was deeply rooted in the United States though of English origin. His father was an engineer and Brown started work as an engineering apprentice with Westinghouse in Manchester.

When war broke out he felt himself sufficiently British to renounce his citizenship and join the Army in September 1914, enlisting in a University and Public Schools battalion of Kitchener's Army. Brown was commissioned in the Manchester Regiment in January 1915 and was in the trenches in France that year.

He then transferred to the Royal Flying Corps as an observer. He was shot down twice, the second time over enemy territory. With his pilot, the famous escaper Captain Medlicott whom the Germans later murdered, he was made prisoner, Brown with a leg injury. After fourteen months in Germany he was exchanged into Switzerland where he spent nine months before repatriation to non-combatant work on aircraft engine construction in December 1917.

While in captivity Brown made a study of aerial navigation, which was then in a very rudimentary state, and devised methods which avoided the need for the visual sightings of landmarks. He tried his ideas on firms who were entering for the *Daily Mail* prize but getting no encouragement gave up the idea until, when applying to Vickers for an engineering job, he met Alcock and his

Telegram announcing departure.
(Vickers)

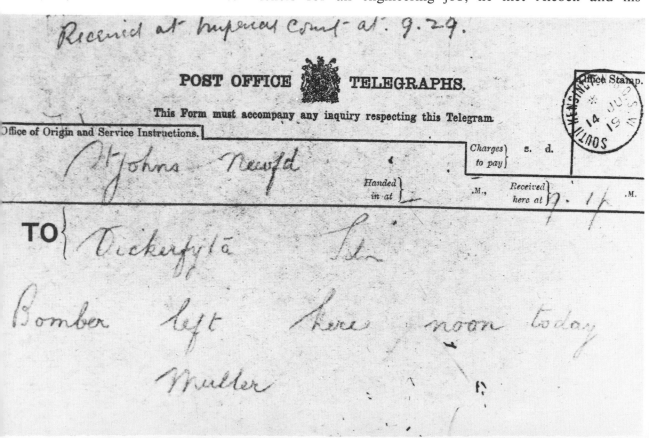

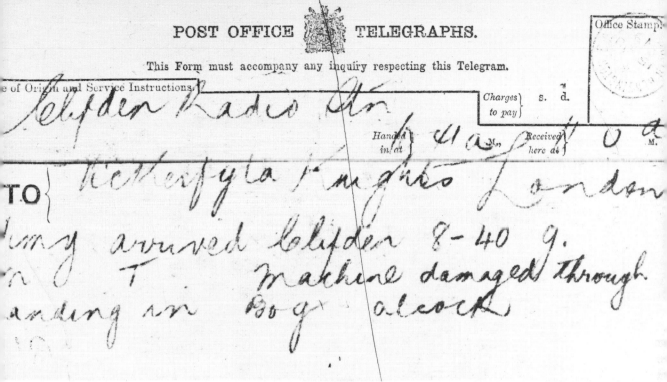

Telegram announcing arrival.
(Vickers)

navigational skill became apparent. The Vickers team was complete.

Bob Dicker, who was born near to the Brooklands track, had worked with the distinguished Granville Bradshaw of ABC motor-cycle fame before World War I. He joined the Vickers aircraft factory during the war and became an expert rigger and a specialist in Bowden wire controls. Jack Alcock, who knew Dicker and his skill, asked for him to be included in the ground crew to go to Newfoundland to rebuild the Vimy.

Dicker tells us that on arrival they were made very welcome by the Misses Dooleys, the owners of the Cochrane Hotel where the Sopwith and Martinsyde teams also lodged. The first difficulty was in finding a flat strip of ground long enough for the Vimy to take off, as being the last to arrive they found the best sites already taken. The difficulty was solved by Raynham's crash on 18 May. When they moved the Martinsyde into St John's for repairs Raynham offered the Vickers crew the use of his strip and tent at Quidi Vidi field.

The plane arrived on 26 May and after much trouble the big crates, over 30 ft long, were manoeuvred out to Quidi Vidi by Mr Lester and his team of horse-drawn floats. Uncrating began at once, just as the biting cold rains came down.

The Vimy was much bigger than Raynham's Martinsyde and the tent would only hold the tail so work had to be done in the open. Wind-breaks with tarpaulins were made; it was perishing cold as Dicker said, and if that wasn't enough, over came the Handley Page on a test flight from Harbour Grace about 80 miles away.

As time was crucial, Dicker and Montgomery decided to sleep on

Front page of the 'New York Herald'. (Vickers)

the job to cut out delays, and used two of the crates for a sleeping and a dining hut. The erecting finished on 9 June and the Vimy with a light load was flown across to Lester's field about three miles off, where Mr Lester, the carter, had put a strip of land at their disposal, putting on a gang to clear the bigger rocks that littered the field. The Vimy needed a run of about 500 yards and this was created. From here a single brief test flight was made on 12 June as Alcock was eager to fly on the 13th, his lucky number.

They were unable to leave on the 13th for when the ground crew had fully loaded the machine with 870 gallons of petrol and 40 gallons of oil, a list to one side was seen. It appeared that the strain was too much for one axle shock absorber. So working all night the team carried out the repairs needed.

On Saturday, 14 June everything was ready for the attempt although the machine had never flown fully loaded. Dicker was helping Brown into his kit, because of his injured leg, when Alcock beckoned him over and said 'Come on Bob, get these engines started, it's time to go'.

Dicker goes on: 'I shall never forget that take-off. I can hardly put into words my feelings as I saw the Vimy at about 100 yards from the end of the strip still firmly on the ground, heading straight for a low thick stone wall . . . Suddenly the Vimy rose about five feet, dropped and then bumped over the wall with about two feet to spare. I believe to this day that someone other than an earthly being handled that joy-stick at that last moment. Once over the wall nature took a hand as the ground immediately fell away into a deep valley . . . I felt certain that they must be down in the woods that

The Vickers 'Vimy' nose-down in an Irish bog (Vickers)

now blocked our view . . . but there was a wonderful moment to come. Freddy Raynham yelled, 'Look Bob!' and behold there was the Vimy coming through a gap in the hills going like an SE5 fighter. They must have been doing 130 mph with a machine with a top speed of around 90 mph — some wind. What a marvellous sight it was as they flew over us, waving vigorously and heading for the sea and success'.[1]

Bob Dicker's story ends on a good note. He said: 'What a Sunday morning to remember. We received a Westinghouse cablegram as follows: 'We did not let you down. Alcock and Brown'. To me that message was proof enough of the high esteem they held for our co-operation in the entire operation. I very much regret that the cablegram was lost and is not available for all to see'. It is pleasing to report that this cablegram came to light in the Penn-Gaskell collection at the Science Museum during the research for this book, and Bob Dicker was able to have a photocopy before he died.

[1]*Transport Pioneers of the 20th Century.* The Transport Trust (Patrick Stephens) 1981.

Statues of Alcock and Brown at Heathrow. (Vickers)

The flight itself followed the normal pattern: the almost immediate failure of the wireless, variable cloud and weather occasionally clear and towering unscalable clouds, fog, rain, sleet and snow at higher altitudes. Alcock never took his hands and feet from the controls and at times flew high and at times flew low to escape the worst of the weather.

On one moment in cloud the Vimy stalled and spun down and only emerged at a frightening angle to the sea about 100 ft up, but Alcock righted her in time. So the hours wore on, Alcock constantly flying and Brown preoccupied with their position. However, he got enough 'sights' for his sextant to show that their position need arouse no anxiety as they were never seriously off course.

One unpleasant task fell to Brown; at a height of 8500 ft he found that the glass face of the petrol flow gauge on one of the centre struts was obscured by snow. It was essential that this gauge should be clearly readable to know that the supply of petrol to the engines was correct. So Brown had to hoist himself up in his seat, kneel on the edge of the fuselage, hang on in the bitter 100 mph airstream and clear the gauge. This grim task was repeated half a dozen times. It has also given rise to the myth that Brown, bad leg and all, had walked on the wings to clear this gauge or the carburettors, the pitot tube, the radiators or other blocked gauges. As if what he did was not enough; just to see the machine shows that wing-walking at 100 mph was impossible.

On the whole, the engines behaved splendidly as they normally did in those days, and only gave one moment of anxiety just before the wonderful, superlative moment when Alcock sighted the small islands of Eashal and Turbot off the Irish coast at 08.15 GMT on the morning of Sunday 15 June. The journey had occupied 16 hours and 28 minutes for approximately 1860 miles. The coast-to-coast time was 15 hours 57 minutes.

The rest is anticlimax: the landing in a bog, the incredulity of the inhabitants of Clifden, breakfast and the journey to Galway. Then

Triumphant arrival in London.
(Vickers)

'New York Tribune' headlines.
(Vickers)

followed adulation, hero-worship and rewards. Alcock's first comment on the flight to journalists was 'We have had a terrible journey' but during the first moments after landing at Clifden his feelings were less extreme, even nonchalant, according to Graham Wallace's account; later on he was inclined to understatement about what must have been a hair-raising experience.

The King sent his congratulations, so did the President of the United States and the Prime Minister, and so did many famous persons of the day; a visit to Windsor came on 21 June for the men to be Knighted.

At the lunch at which the £10,000 cheque was presented Winston Churchill, the Minister of War and Air, was in fine form. He said:

> 'We are met together to celebrate a most wonderful and valiant achievement . . . In 1492 Christopher Columbus sailed across the Atlantic and discovered America. I cannot help feeling that this afternoon we are to some extent in contact with and in relation to that event . . . Think of the broad Atlantic, that terrible waste

72

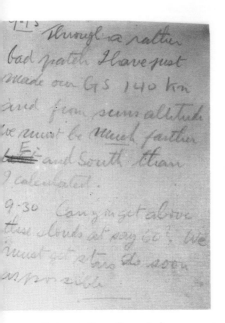

Extracts from Brown's log. (Vickers)

of desolate water tossing to tumult in repeated and almost ceaseless storms and shrouded with an unbroken canopy of mist. Across this waste and through this obscurity, two human beings hurtling through the air, piercing the clouds and darkness, finding their unerring path in spite of every difficulty, to their exact objective on schedule time and at every moment in this voyage liable to destruction . . . They are the real victors. It is no disparagement to the gallantry of Mr. Hawker. It is no disparagement to the brilliantly executed exploits of the United States Navy which working along Service lines have obtained results of extraordinary value from a Service point of view. It is no disparagement to any of these gallant and skilful efforts, if we say in surveying the Atlantic flight made by Alcock and Brown 'This is it!'

The American Ambassador also spoke very handsomely and the proposal was put to the United States Congress by Representative Fiorello La Guardia, later New York's famous mayor, that they should be awarded the Congressional Medal of Honor. No one could say that American tributes were not generous. The *New York Times* published a poem of four stanzas by Lewis Edward Collings, the last of which read:

> 'Hail! gallant birdmen
> Laurel your crown
> Glorious pilots
> Alcock and Brown'

Winston Churchill presenting the 'Daily Mail' £10,000 cheque.
(Associated Newspapers)

Rob Dicker, motorcycle record breaker 1922.
(R. E. Dicker)

Flight's editorial said:

'It is with the profoundest satisfaction that we are able to record the fact that the first direct flight across the Atlantic has been accomplished by British aviators, flying a British machine which is British in design and construction down to the last detail — not forgetting the engine. By their successful crossing of the wild Atlantic Capt. Alcock and Lieut. Brown have achieved a performance which will remain a landmark in history throughout the ages and have placed to the credit of Britain and her sons a record second to none in the story of achievement by land, sea and air . . . In paying tribute to the wonderful performance of Alcock and Brown, we do not discount for a moment the almost equally glorious failure of Hawker and Grieve, or the more successful though less spectacular performance of Lieut. Commander Read and his crew. Indeed in so far as the latter is concerned nothing can alter the fact that to America belongs the glory of having been the first to throw an aerial bridge across the Atlantic . . . Still it is

Vickers 'Vimy', conqueror of the Atlantic.
(Science Museum)

the names of Alcock and Brown which will be forever associated with the first direct crossing, and we scarcely think it is claiming too much to ask that they should be credited with the first real Atlantic flight'.

Perhaps it is fair to bring in the verdict of an impartial referee, Maurice Bellonte of the French team of Costes and Bellonte who flew non-stop from Paris to New York for the first time in 1939. In a French aviation journal Bellonte wrote:

Erecting the 'Vimy' in Newfoundland. (Vickers)

'Trois étapes et onze jours pour franchir les 4000 Km de Terre-Neuve à Lisbonne, c'est encore bien loin de la traversée directe et, en égard aux moyens mis en oeuvre et

Photocopy of the 'Daily Mail'
page. (Daily Mail)

à la perte de deux hydravions sur trois, qui ont dû être abandonnés, en mer, heureusement sans perte de vies humaines, le résultat n'est guère probant.

Par cette traversée directe, l'Angleterre vient de mettre a son actif la première et nette victoire de l'avion sur L'Atlantique nord[1].

---

[1]In the Summer 1977 issue of *Icare*: 'Three stages and eleven days to cross the 2500 miles from Newfoundland to Lisbon is a long way from a direct crossing, and considering the effort made and the loss of two planes out of three, which had to be abandoned at sea, fortunately without loss of life, the result is hardly convincing.

By this direct crossing, England has gained the asset of the first clear victory of the aeroplane over the North Atlantic.'

ANGLO-AMERICAN TELEGRAPH COMPANY, LIMITED

CONNECTING WITH
THE WESTERN UNION TELEGRAPH COMPANY

ST. JOHN'S N.F
JUN 16 1919

Q36Z   MARCONI........

CLIFDEN RADIO STN 22

VICKERS MECHANICS

STJOHNSNFLD—

YOUR HARD WORK AND SPLENDID EFFORTS HAVE BEEN AMPLY REWARDED STOP WE DID

NOT LET YOU DOWN.

ALCOCK BROWN.

No inquiry respecting this Message can be attended to without the production of this paper.

Telegram to the ground crew.
(Science Museum)

The story's end is a sad one, John Alcock, ferrying a new Vickers amphibian machine, a Viking, to Paris for the Air Salon on 18 December 1919, crashed in bad weather near Rouen and was killed.

Arthur Whitten Brown, it is said, never flew again after Alcock's death. He married and lived a quiet life in Swansea until he died in 1948; their only son was killed flying over Arnhem during World War II. Sadly Brown died by his own hand, by misadventure, taking accidentally an overdose of sleeping pills which had been prescribed after he had had a nervous breakdown.

The Vimy never flew again. It was given to the nation and is well displayed in the Science Museum.

Perhaps the best judgement on this epic flight is the that no one successfully matched it for eight years, until Lindbergh flew from New York to Paris in the *Spirit of St Louis*.

6.
British Zeppelin

The history of British airships is not distinguished; a story of too little and too late, of rashness and timidity, of interference and indifference, of parsimony and extravagance, of quality and achievement and of bungling and ignorance.

When they lost the war in November 1918 the Germans had been consistently ahead of the world in the design, construction and use of airships until the weapons which ultimately destroyed them had so improved as to put a stop to their most memorable activities, the terrorist raids on England. Nevertheless, the British Government, impressed by the German Zeppelins, especially their value as naval scouts, pursued a policy of rigid airship construction with a mixture of economy and extravagance which virtually made certain that we would never catch up. It is perhaps a surprise to realise that no fewer than twenty British rigid airships were laid down between the R1 the *Mayfly,* of 1911 — which never did — and the R101 of 1929. True

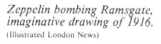

Zeppelin bombing Ramsgate, imaginative drawing of 1916.
(Illustrated London News)

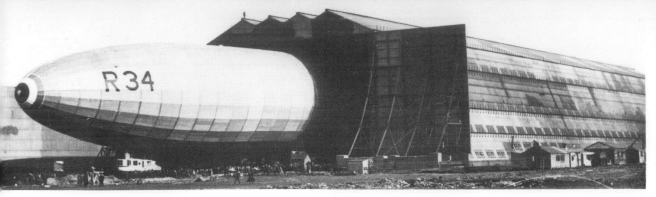

The airship being walked-out of its hangar.
(Royal Aeronautical Society)

the R35 and the R37 were not completed and the R39 was cancelled, but the remainder were completed though some, like the wooden-framed R31 and the metal-framed R36, hardly flew at all.

After the failure of the Vickers-built *Mayfly,* which broke her back at Barrow-in-Furness in a gust of wind without becoming airborne, no one in Britain was in a hurry to try again in spite of the fact that Zeppelins in Germany were running a commercial air service as early as 1910. However, in March 1914 Vickers were ordered to build another rigid airship, the R9, and it was in this construction that Barnes Wallis first became engaged in aviation. The work proceeded haltingly and it was April 1917 before the R9 was handed over to the Navy. She was designed from first principles and turned out to be a small but useful airship of 880,000 cubic feet. Less good was the subsequent 20-Class which was built to plans which had been pieced together from the residues of German Zeppelins shot down over England; the design lacked German experience and aerodynamical knowledge. There were seven of these, R23-29 — the first four completed in 1917 — and they were inferior performers, lacking lift and speed and useful only for training and mooring experiments though R29 did help to destroy a German submarine. The R31 and R32 were wooden-framed airships intended to match the German Schütte-Lanz design but it seems R31 only flew twice, though R32 had a more useful life.

In contrast to this rather dismal story of the British non-rigid airships of World War I, the Coastal, North Sea, S.S. and C-Star types did good and useful work on escort and anti-submarine patrols.

It was only when we got hold of a German Zeppelin almost intact in September 1916 that our designers had enough to go on to be able to make an exact copy and build Britain's first successful rigid

The end of the airship, with its damaged nose, 1921. (Royal Aeronautical Society)

Wreckage of the L.33 at Little Wigborough, 24th September 1916.
(Associated Newspapers)

Lt. Böcker, captain of the L.33, briefly in command of the only disciplined enemy force on British soil since 1797.
(Associated Newspapers)

airships of a useful size, the R33 and R34. The German L33, with two sister ships, had raided London on the night of 23/24 September 1916. L32 was shot down in flames and all on board perished; L31 escaped but was lost on the next raid with the most famous Zeppelin commander, Mathy, on board. L33, after dropping bombs on the East End of London, was damaged by anti-aircraft fire from guns at Beckton and Wanstead and began to lose gas; an engine was damaged and one shell had passed clean through the airship. After this Flt. Lt. Brandon, in a BE2C biplane, attacked the airship and riddled it with bullets at close range. The combined effects of our retaliation had the L33 in real trouble, so with all movables jettisoned, with labouring engines and badly holed, she grounded at Little Wigborough, just inland from West Mersea in Essex. There was too little gas in the airship to burn much and only the envelope suffered. Capt. Böcker and his men formed up, the only disciplined armed force to land in Britain in two world wars, indeed since the French invasion of Wales in 1797, and started to march towards the coast. However, Constable Nicholas on his bicycle soon put a stop to that and led them unprotesting to the local police station where they were formally arrested.

The carcase of the L33 was studied in great detail and it became clear that she was far in advance of anything that our designers had so far imagined.

Two copies were ordered, the R33 to be built by Armstrong-Whitworth and the R34 by William Beardmore & Co at Inchinnan near Glasgow: three more of the same design were intended. The design followed exactly the German pattern except for the number, disposal and make of the engines.

So two of Britain's most successful airships came into being; the R33 having a useful and unspectacular career, once surviving a

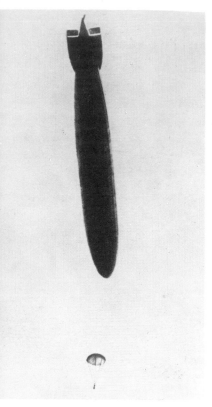

The first overseas visitor to arrive in the U.S.A. by air; Major Pritchard descending by parachute. (Illustrated London News)

The R.34 starts for home, lit by searchlights of its American hosts. (Smithsonian Institution)

badly damaged forward section while in flight and remaining in service until she was finally dismantled in 1924 after flying 1000 hours. It was only when our designers, lacking aerodynamical knowledge, scaled up the R33/34 design to make a larger airship, the R38 which broke her back in trials, that their ignorance was apparent. R33's sister, the R34, by flying the Atlantic both ways, making the first east to west flight and the first round trip, will be the only airship that lives in British memory other than the disastrous failure, the R101. But for the R101 disaster, the fine R100 designed by Barnes Wallis and built by private enterprise or even his beautiful small R80 might have become famous. At least the R100 was able to make a double Atlantic crossing before the Government in a fit of panic, broke her up and sold the scrap for £450.

The German L33 which we had captured was fortunately the most modern in the German airship fleet at that time, although surpassed by later types, so that our copies were away to a good start. With a gas volume of 1,950,000 cubic feet the R34 was far bigger than any airship we had yet built and as all the accounts point out, had an overall length of 643 ft, twice as long as a football pitch. Her gasbags contained 4.8 tons of hydrogen which displaced 69 tons of air so that she was rated as having a gross lift of 59 tons or disposable lift after allowing for her structure and engines of 26 tons.

The power plant was five 12-cylinder Sunbeam Maori 4 engines, one attached to the rear of the forward control cabin, two amidships in gondolas on either side of the airship, and two together in an engine-car towards the tail. The nominal horse power of the engines was 250 which was intended to provide a maximum speed of 62 mph. It seems that this power was never attained and R34 was almost certainly chronically under-powered. The various parts of the ship were connected by a narrow walkway 600 ft long inside the frame and there was also access to the top of the envelope.

The British Government had been approached by the Aero Club of America in March 1919 asking that an airship should be sent to take part in a meeting at Atlantic City in May, the Americans having no rigid airships at that time. With our airships only completed in

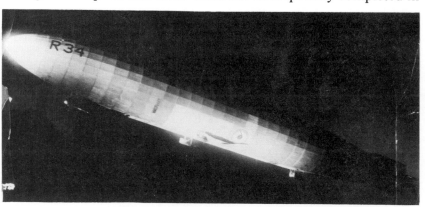

The R.34 with its hydrogen cylinders at Mineola, Long Island, U.S.A. (Smithsonian Institution)

December 1918 and not yet having done trials, it was impossible to meet the May date, but the idea of a transatlantic voyage was accepted and it was agreed that the newly formed RAF would borrow the naval R34 for a trip to the United States and back in the summer.

Trials started in mid-March and on an extended flight on 24 March some difficulties were met in the air after which the R34 narrowly escaped a serious crash landing. After repairs, the airship left Inchinnan at the end of May for her Station at East Fortune near Edinburgh. From there she carried out a long trial flight over Germany, the Baltic, southern Sweden and Norway, during which she was armed, and by the end of June was ready for the Atlantic.

Normally a crew of 22 was the complement of the R34 but for the long Atlantic voyage Major Scott, the Captain, put on board two extra men for additional maintenance and flying duties and three extra officers for radio, meteorological and navigating duties. An American naval officer was invited to come as an observer and there was also an observer for the Admiralty. The most senior passenger was Brigadier-General Edward Maitland though he was not in command. Although this was a naval airship and the ship's company consisted of Air Force men, they still held Army ranks as the new RAF had not yet worked out its designations of rank. Scott, who had been an RNAS Lieutenant-Commander, became a Major although he wore the new RAF head-dress which at that time carried 'scrambled egg' on the peak.

The R.34 returning to England.
(BBC/Hulton)

Patrick Abbott's *Airship* lists the crew as follows:

Major G. H. Scott, AFC	Captain
Capt. G. S. Greenland	Second officer
2nd Lt. H. F. Luck	Third officer
Major G. C. H. Cooke, DSC	Navigator
2nd Lt. J. D. Shotter	Engineering officer
Lt. G. Harris	Meteorological officer
2nd Lt. H. F. Durrant	Wireless officer
Brig. Gen. E. M. Maitland	
Major J. E. M. Pritchard, OBE	Observer for Admiralty
Lt. Cmdr. Z. Lansdowne, USN	Observer for US Navy
W.O.2 W. R. Mayes	First coxswain
Flt. Sgt. W. J. Robinson	Second coxswain

Engineers
Flt. Sgt. W. R. Gent
Flt. Sgt. N. A. Scull
Flt. Sgt. R. W. Ripley
Sgt. A. G. Evenden
Sgt. J. Thirlwall
Cpl. E. P. Cross
Cpl. J. H. Gray
LAC G. Graham
LAC J. S. Mort
AC2 J. Northeast
AC2 R. Parker

Riggers
Sgt. H. M. Watson
Cpl. R. J. Burgess
Cpl. F. Smith
LAC F. P. Browdie
LAC J. N. Forteath

Wireless operators
Cpl. H. P. Powell
AC1 W. J. Edwards

Three airmen who had flown with the ship so far were left behind to save weight, also Major Scott's dog, but a kitten destined to become famous was smuggled aboard and made the round trip. There was also a stowaway on board, of whom more in a moment, who made the total up to 31 and two carrier pigeons from East Fortune though no one seems to know why. One pigeon made the round trip with the airship but the other escaped and was rescued heading for home and exhausted by S.S. *West Kyska* which was 1100 miles out in the Atlantic from Baltimore.

With the extra men on board Major Scott took on only 4900 gallons of petrol, 1100 gallons less than the R34's capacity and this decision nearly ruined the whole enterprise for when the airship reached New York she had only enough fuel for another three or four hours' flying at reduced power. Even the extra fifteen gallons represented by the stowaway would have been welcome then.

So at 1.42 am GMT on 2 July 1919 Scott called 'Let go', a bugle call rang out into the sharp night air and R34 was off on the first east to west flight with a huge White Ensign at her tail. Almost at once she was lost in the clouds and could only sense the presence of an army of well-wishers by the faint noise of the cheers which penetrated through to the airship.

The last of Europe was seen later that morning, at Rathlin Island on the north coast of Ulster, and R34 forged on at a leisurely 45-50 mph with 2000 miles of open sea ahead towards the coast of Newfoundland.

On the morning of 2 July when R34 was nosing out into the Atlantic the stowaway was discovered, AC2 William Ballantyne, a 22-year-old rigger, one of those excluded at the last moment. He had been in the Royal Naval Air Service since 1915, training on balloons and then on airships.

It was somehow an eerie experience for me to be able to meet and interview Ballantyne, then a little old man of 80 but still with vivid memories to be dug out by questioning[1]. He had served with the R34 throughout her trials, including the voyage over the Baltic, and so was dismayed when he found his name left off the roster for the Atlantic. He resolved not to take no for an answer and stowed away around 10.00 pm in the evening on which the airship was due to leave, by the simple method of mixing with and helping the ground crew who were loading stores aboard the airship. The guards knew him as a member of the crew so he aroused no suspicions. At a suitable moment he dodged out of sight and hid himself on a girder between gasbags six and seven above the crew's quarters.

Silence fell, then he heard the crew come aboard. Then Ballantyne heard the command to the ground crew in the hangar. As he told it: 'I heard the order "Ease off the guys. Hands off". and the ship lifted slightly and R34 was in the hands of the ground crew holding ropes

[1]See the Transport Trust's verbatim account in *Transport Pioneers of the 20th Century.* Patrick Stephens, 1981.

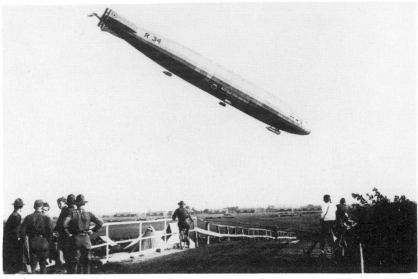

R.34 preparing to land in U.S.A.
(Royal Aeronautical Society)

attached to the ship.' Then, he said, 'After the command "Walk the ship ahead" I heard the heavy footsteps of the 200 men walking the ship out of the shed. Next came the command "Let go" and we were away, to the multitude of cheers from the ground'. Ballantyne had intended to stay hidden for the whole voyage if possible but hydrogen from the relief valves made him sick so that he had to move to a more open place. Here, about five hours out, he was discovered.

One member of the crew resented his presence and complained 'He'll eat our grub', but others said, 'He can have half of mine'. So he resolved to eat no food other than his own two sandwiches on the voyage. Major Scott, who was a kindly man, half smiled and told Ballantyne he'd have to get to work, which he did. After he'd recovered from the hydrogen poisoning he worked his passage but was not one of those who made the round trip.

The New York reporters discovered that he was a boxer and had been an RAF open champion. The *New York Times* disclosed that he would not have minded having a bout for a purse while in America.

Contrary to one account, when Ballantyne returned home by the *Aquitania* to England, he escaped court martial — by General Maitland's intervention he thought. He was reprimanded by his station commander and 'dismissed his ship', that is put back on ground duties. Shortly afterwards Major Scott got him posted to the airship R80 and later obtained for him his arrears of flying pay, two shillings a day for the period in which he had been grounded. General Maitland gave him a copy of his book saying, 'Here you are, naughty boy'. Ballantyne in interview was sure that his escapade had not got him into any black book, or ruined his career.

He remained with the RAF, learned to fly on an Avro, and from Warrant Officer Pilot via Sergeant Pilot he was commissioned and

An early aerial stowaway, William Ballantyne with the ship's cat in America. (Press Associaton)

served in World War II ending as a Flight Lieutenant. He was twice mentioned in dispatches, first for good work in Iraq in the twenties and then again for good work in France in 1940 with a Fairey Battle squadron.

All through the first day R34 pushed ahead through fog, rain, mist and clouds with occasional clear weather, but next day the wind rose and the airship had to fight her way westward. The engines were none too reliable and had to have periods of rest. A cracked cylinder water jacket was repaired aloft with copper tape and chewing gum. Wireless contact was maintained throughout the flight and weather reports were received from the battle-cruisers *Tiger* and *Renown*.

Land was sighted about 1.30 pm GMT on 4 July and finally at 4.30 pm GMT R34 passed over Fortune Harbour in Newfoundland and the first east to west crossing was accomplished. This flight of 59 hours would have been within the time limit of 72 hours set for the *Daily Mail* prize though far slower than Alcock and Brown's flight less than three weeks before.

Life on board was unexciting with naval watchkeeping practice of four hours on duty and off with dog-watches. Cold meals were the rule with an occasional hot dish or cup of tea heated on the hot plate attached to the exhaust pipe of one engine. It is an interesting commentary on changing habits to read in General Maitland's log: 'We would one and all give anything for a smoke'. Today probably fewer than half would say that.

After passing over Newfoundland that evening R34 crossed the French islands of St. Pierre and Miquelon, the last remains of the French empire in Canada, and the tricolor was ceremonially lowered on shore but alas the White Ensign astern was too remote for the honour to be returned. That evening too they picked up the radio of the Handley Page V1500 which had left Newfoundland disappointed of the *Daily Mail* prize and bound also for New York. The unlucky Raynham also wirelessed that he had repaired his Martinsyde and was coming up to escort the airship — he didn't make it. That night, the 4th of July, fortified by the news that Jack Dempsey had just won the heavyweight championship of the world, the R34 had to fight increasing head winds and rough weather. During the Saturday, 5 July, Major Scott chose to fly very low, so low that barking dogs could be heard, which made the stowaway cat bristle, and the sweet smell of warm pine trees came up to the airship from the Nova Scotia woods where as Maitland noted: 'The stacked tree trunks looked like bunches of asparagus from above put end up'. They saw a big brown eagle too.

By the afternoon of 5 July, petrol was becoming a major anxiety and Scott feared he might have to come down at Boston to refuel or else refuel at sea or, worst of all, accept a tow from a warship. After weathering two thunderstorms that night it appeared that the ship could manage to pass Boston but would have to land at Montauk at the eastern tip of Long Island to refuel. To take care of this possibility 200 men had been sent to Montauk with supplies of petrol and hydrogen, but just in time a following wind came up and Scott was able to risk going all the way to their intended destination at Roosevelt Field, Mineola, at the New York City end of Long Island. The *New York Times* reported: 'At 8.35 o'clock the R34 became visible from Mineola Field looking at first like a splinter split off from the bluish horizon to the North-East'. So at 9.54 am local time (1.54 pm GMT) with, according to the *New York Times,* 'the band playing "God save the King" and thousands of spectators standing bareheaded', the R34 touched earth after spending 108 hours and 12 minutes in the air, slightly longer than the record by sea of the *Mauretania,* with only 140 gallons of petrol left, which Scott did not think gave him enough in hand to let him fly over New York City before landing.

If the voyage had been relatively uneventful the moment of arrival was spectacular. Grover Loening, the American aircraft manufacturer, wrote[1]:

'My first experience with the so-called 'rigid' airships occurred when I happened to be at Roosevelt Field, L.I.,

Major Scott who commanded the R.34. He later lost his life in the R.101 disaster.

[1]*Take Off into Greatness,* Grover Loening. Putnam, 1968.

Model of the R.34 displayed at Heathrow with five R.34 survivors in 1962: l to r Ballantyne, Browdie, Gray, Smith, Parker.
(Associated Newspapers)

on July 6 1919 to see the arrival of the giant after its crossing of the Atlantic. The speed of the crossing was not too impressive, but the landing was. As the ship floated stationary over the field at an altitude of 1000 ft, a sudden burst of white fell from its control cabin. In a moment the object opened into a parachute and with a sangfroid and a chic that only the English can put over, the executive officer of the R.34, Squadron Leader Pritchard, landed lightly and unconcerned in full beribboned uniform, carrying a swagger stick! Efficiently he commanded the landing operations. Then a long process of warping the ship down to tie-downs, with the crew of 30 and several eager helpers holding on. I was able to examine it quite closely; my first impression was how 'unrigid' it really was. In photos and when first seen it seemed a massively strong structure justifying the name of 'rigid'. But close up one was astounded to see how the frame squeaked, bent and shivered with the cloth covering almost flapping in wind gusts . . . The next day a storm came up and again I was a witness. Lighter than air it certainly was. And the air knew it! I was shocked at its flimsiness and the wicked wrenching of the gusts. The wind gusts seemed so severe that the whole works seemed likely to be wrecked any moment. Frantically the crew and many others tugged and pulled on ropes and handrails to restrain the monster in its unwieldy gyrations. As for the shivering and shaking of the 'rigid' structure, it so shocked me that from that day on I could not put my faith in these storm-vulnerable, expensive and to me highly impractical 'pigs' . . . I left with no desire to see it again'.

The newspapers account said that Pritchard, the first overseas visitor to reach the United States by air, jumped from 2000 feet and took two minutes to come down swinging round and round in circles; he landed rather heavily, hurting his hip.

Loening's description of the flimsiness and unmanageability of the huge vessels certainly may come as a surprise though it is supported by accounts published at the time. My personal recollections of these huge flying machines — the R33 seen once, the

Engines of the R.33; R.34's were similar. (National Motor Museum)

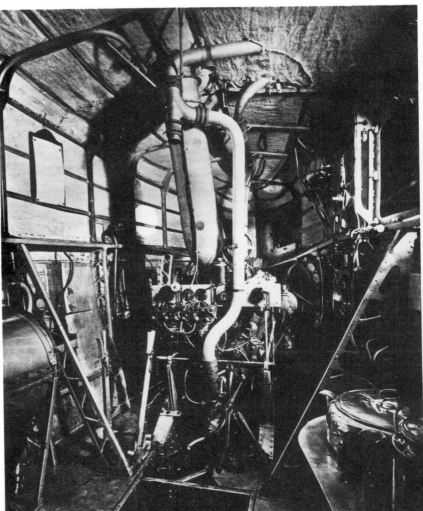

'New York Times' salutations.
(New York Times)

R100 and the R101 over London in 1930 and once the *Hindenburg* out in mid-Atlantic in 1936 — are that they seemed creatures of massive strength and stability but of course in fact they were atrociously vulnerable, unwieldy and unpractical. Indeed, it took 600 men to get the R34 moored and 800 men were permanently on hand at Mineola during her stay. In her descent we read that coming down really fast at 300 feet the R34 'suddenly released a great flood of water ballast which spread into a sheet and then poured in a torrent to the ground showering the workmen under it'. A few minutes later, when the main cable had been secured, 'the crews of men were pinning it down like Gulliver'. Yet these handicaps were not recognised as decisive at the time and the use of mooring masts greatly aided docking. The airship was favoured because the large aeroplane was not yet advanced enough to be even a threat to these great gasbags. Only a series of disasters culminating in the hideous destruction of the *Hindenburg* in full public view in 1937 closed the chapter. Our own book was shut in 1930 when the R101 was wrecked at Beauvais with the Air Minister, Lord Thomson, Air Vice-Marshal Sir Sefton Brancker and, of the R34's crew, Major Scott and W. R. Gent all killed along with 44 others. Similarly, Air Commodore Maitland, Aircraftman Parker and Wing Commander Pritchard from the R34 perished with 41 others in the wreck of the R38, including the unlucky Commander Coil, USN, who had been the captain of the US airship C5 lost in Newfoundland in 1919, and Lt. Charles G. Little of the C5's ground crew.

So the euphoria and expectations produced by the flight of the R34, enhanced by later German successes with the LZ126 and the *Graf Zeppelin,* came to be overtaken by disillusion and the age of the airship died. Whether a slower and more painstaking development and the use of helium instead of hydrogen to provide lift would have kept the big airship alive is questionable.

The R34's stay in the United States was marked by an outpouring of enthusiasm, friendship and hospitality which only Americans can provide. A thousand dollars was offered and refused for the ship's cat and altogether the press had a field day.

For the return flight, the stowaway Ballantyne was excluded, Lt. Cmdr. Lansdowne of the US Navy gave way to Lt. Col. W. N. Hemsley of the US Army and one of the wireless operators AC1 Edwards, was put off so that Scott could take on two more engineers to help sustain the ailing motors. These were Flt. Sgts. Turner and Angus from the advance party which had gone to New York by sea. Thus the total of those returning was 31 with three new names, so that in all 28 men made the round trip and six made a single journey.

The return journey, starting just before midnight on 9 July, like most return journeys was something of an anticlimax. R34 cruised over New York after midnight, noting the myriad lights of Times Square, Broadway and Fifth Avenue, and was seen by thousands of upturned faces. Then with good following wind she boomed back

Cheering the R.34 home at Pulham. (Press Association)

across the Atlantic on a more southerly route, crossing — in 61 hours and 33 minutes out of New York — the Irish coast exactly where Alcock and Brown had first seen land. In 75 hours and three minutes, in spite of some engine trouble including losing one engine completely, the R34 docked at Pulham in Norfolk discharging, just as the band struck up 'See the conquering hero comes', the rest of her water ballast and spare water. The most attractive moment of the return flight must have been when the R34 sighted a five-masted schooner in full sail alone in the huge Atlantic.

The return of the R34 was somehow a non-event; it was as if the supply of British enthusiasm was exhausted by the exploits of Hawker and Mackenzie Grieve and of Alcock and Whitten Brown. Few decorations were given or rewards made, although they brought back gold medals for Alcock and Brown from the Aero Club of America. It was all rather sad, like the end of this famous airship, wrecked after storm damage in 1921.

As a nation we seem to prefer desperate deeds of derring-do, which Alcock and Brown's exploit was seen to be, even if they end in gallant failure like Hawker and Grieve's flight, rather than efficient operations like the R34's apparently faultless performance or the

American naval flying boat exercise. The Americans only enjoy success and regard a good second place with disdain. If success is accompanied by an attractive personality like Lindbergh that is wildly acclaimed. The French too have a surprising taste for gallant failure, as this quotation about 1927, Lindbergh's year, shows: 'La France, qui a toujours un faible pour l'exploit malheureux, commémore cette année la cinquantième anniversaire de la disparition de Charles Nungesser et François Coli[1]'.

The most essential reading for more details of the R34 can be found in Patrick Abbott's admirable book[2] and General Maitland's dispatches published in *Flight* immediately after the double journey.

[1]'France, which always has a weakness for the unfortunate event, commemorates this year (1977) the fiftieth anniversary of the loss of Charles Nungesser and François Coli'. Raymond Nivet in the journal *Icare*.
[2]*Airship* by Patrick Abbott. Adams & Dart, 1973.

7.
Portuguese Perseverance

After the tremendous events of 1919 in which the Atlantic was conquered four times and in which a flight from Britain to Australia had also been accomplished, the next two years were by comparison limited. There were no prizes for being second, indeed no prizes at all were available. No one tried to fly the Atlantic in 1920 or 1921.

Nevertheless it was in 1919 that the first thoughts about flying the South Atlantic were generated, rather surprisingly perhaps in Portugal, though with their earlier fame as discoverers and voyagers it might be expected that the Portuguese would be as likely as any nation to produce skilled navigators. In particular an elderly naval officer with an interest in flying, Captain Carlos Gago Coutinho, had began paying attention to the need for improved instruments for aerial navigation as early as 1917 and by 1919 he had devised and described a new bubble sextant with a built-in artificial horizon which was capable of advising the user with great accuracy. The ordinary sextant required the true horizon to work from; when above clouds, it had serious limitations, although better than the earliest primitive forms of aerial navigation. So the Coutinho instrument was a substantial advance.

Gago Coutinho's early career had been that of a Portuguese naval officer. His parents came from the Algarve and he was born in Belém a suburb of Lisbon on 17 February 1869. He joined the

Modified Fairey IIID seaplane 'Lusitania', the first aircraft used in the crossing. (Flight)

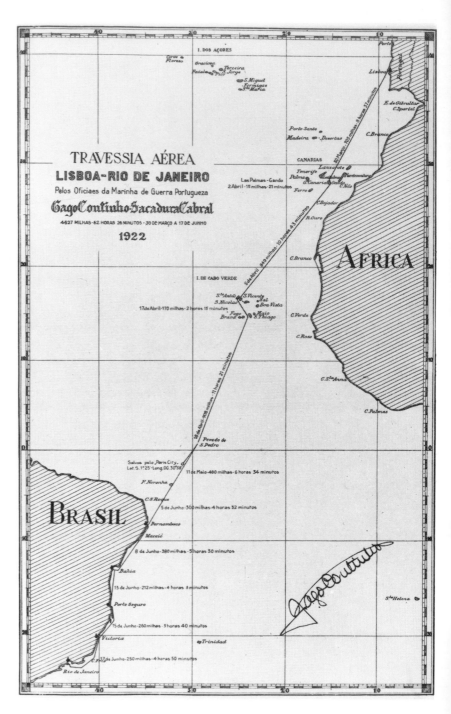

Map of the first South Atlantic crossing. (Flight)

Portuguese navy as a cadet in 1886 reaching the rank of Captain in December 1918. Many years of his service were spent in surveying and geographical work in the Portuguese African colonies, in the course of which he made a double journey of 5200 kilometres on foot across Africa and back. Though not a qualified pilot Gago

Coutinho was interested in flying and received his 'baptismo de voo' in a Maurice Farman at the Military School of Aviation in February 1917 from a naval officer called Sacadura Cabral whom he had met earlier in Africa.

Like Coutinho, Artur de Sacadura Cabral was also a navy career man, born in May 1881; he joined as a cadet in 1897 and reached the rank of Lieutenant-Commander in April 1918. After work in Africa on boundary delimitation and similar activities he was chosen to learn to fly in France at the aviation school at Chartres in 1916. He was then charged with setting up a naval air service and flying school for Portugal by 1919 and was appointed Commander of the Naval Base Squadron at Lisbon. He was also appointed that year to examine aerial navigation and to make a study of the possibility of a flight from Lisbon to Rio de Janeiro, then the capital of Portugal's lost colony, Brazil. If that was not enough Sacadura Cabral was also Air Attaché to the Legations in Paris and London.

Cabral became an enthusiastic and capable airman and, admiring his old colleague's work on navigation and instruments, one of his first tasks was to 'convert him from a pedestrian into an aviator'. Cabral appreciated the value of Coutinho's new sextant and by 1919, when he and his friend had devised a drift-indicator as well, he believed that enough navigational aids were at hand to make the passage of the South Atlantic feasible.

As a first trial Sacadura Cabral proposed a non-stop flight from Lisbon to Madeira, a distance of 530 nautical miles (610 statute miles), using the new instruments. An earlier attempt on this flight was made by Brito Pais, Sarmento de Beires and Jorge de Castilho on 18 October 1920 in a French war-surplus Breguet XIV-A2 with a 300 hp Renault engine. This had failed through an error in navigation which put them down 50 miles south-east of their target.

For his attempt Cabral decided to use one of the two Felixstowe F3 flying boats of Porte's design, which Portugal had obtained from Britain at the end of the war after complete overhaul at Fairey Aviation at Southampton. He had already flown one of these from Calshot to Lisbon in stages. The flight to Madeira was barely within the range of an F3 but with a light following wind it was expected to be attainable.

So on the 22 March 1921 at approximately 10.30 am Cabral took off, this time with Capt. Coutinho as navigator, Lt. Ortins Bettencourt as radio officer and Roger Soubiran, a Frenchman, as mechanic. This time there was no mistake, the navigation was exact and, disdaining the temptation to come down at Porto Santo, 45 sea-miles short of Madeira, they arrived in Funchal Bay 7 hours 40 minutes after leaving Lisbon; the 'Portuguese Sextant' or 'Precision Astrolabe' and the drift-corrector worked splendidly and now Cabral was ready for the big project, the South Atlantic.

The shortest distance across the South Atlantic from the mainland of Africa at Cap Santa Anna to the mainland of South

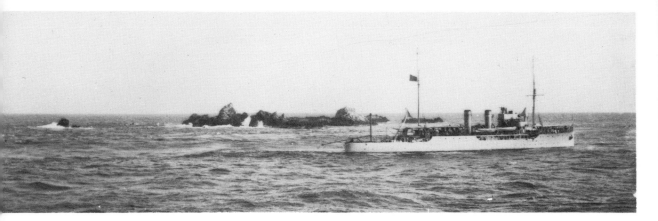

The St. Peter and Paul Rocks in mid-Atlantic with the sloop 'Republica'. (Naval Museum, Lisbon)

America at Cabo Rocque is rather less than the distance from Newfoundland to the coast of Ireland, approximately 1500 nautical miles (1725 statute miles). The weather is usually less severe and variable than in the North Atlantic, the governing features being the north-east trade winds north of the Equator and the south-east trade winds south of the line. So just as the early attacks on the North Atlantic usually took off to fly west to east, to gain advantageous winds, so all the early attempts on the South Atlantic were from east to west to get help from the trade winds.

There are moreover some convenient islands which, like the Azores in the North Atlantic, could serve as stopping places and so cut down the length of the individual stages. These are the Canary Islands and the Cape Verde Islands on the African side and Fernando Noronha on the Brazilian. In addition there are some groups of uninhabited rocks in the South Atlantic such as the Abrolhos Rocks at which the Royal Navy maintained a coaling station before the days of oil fuel[1]. Another group, the St. Peter and Paul rocks close to the Equator and on the course from the Cape Verde Islands to Fernando Noronha, played a part in the first flight across the South Atlantic. The plan made therefore was to attempt the passage in four stages thus:

Lisbon - Las Palmas (Canary)	710 nautical miles = 817 statute miles
Las Palmas - Porto Praia (Cape Verde)	910 nautical miles = 1047 statute miles
Porto Praia - Fernando Noronha	1260 nautical miles = 1449 statute miles
Fernando Noronha - Pernambuco (Recife)	300 nautical miles = 345 statute miles

The route via the islands was decidedly shorter than the possible routes on which a land plane could operate, that is along the African

[1]It was here that Admiral Sturdee's battle-cruiser squadron coaled on their way to the Falkland Islands in 1914 to destroy Graf Spee's squadron.

coast to Dakar or Portuguese Guinea, because it could be broken up into sectors. Flying direct from Dakar or Portuguese Guinea involved a non-stop stretch of 1500 nautical miles at the very least to the coast of mainland Brazil and more likely 1600 nautical miles from and to suitable airfields. Allowing an average speed of 75 knots for a laden land plane in 1921, an endurance of 22 hours was necessary.

Using the islands, the longest sector was 1260 nautical miles between the Cape Verde Islands and Fernando Noronha. Although the hydroplanes then available were slower, with an average speed of not more than 70 knots, the endurance of 18 hours which would be needed argued strongly in favour of a seaplane or a flying boat and the island route.

And so it was decided; but first the money had to be found. Here the Portuguese Government in mid-1921 came up with a sum of £5000 for a flight from Lisbon to Rio.

Cabral then had to choose a machine for the job. With a disposition to buy British and with a special admiration for Rolls-Royce engines, he decided that the choice lay between a modified Vickers Viking amphibian flying boat and a modified Fairey seaplane. The modifications needed for the Vickers flying boat were considerable; a new wing and a new body would have to be designed, whereas Fairey Aviation could more easily produce a machine to the necessary specification based on one of their standard IIID seaplanes, by following closely the design of their modified IIIC seaplane which had been built in 1919 for the North Atlantic attempt. A deal with Fairey's was made easier by the Portuguese Government ordering two additional IIID floatplanes for torpedo-carrying experiments.

Fairey seaplanes Nos. 400, 401 and 402 were therefore ordered in the summer of 1921 with Rolls-Royce Eagle VIII engines of 360 hp. No. 400, the Special, was constructed as a two-seater but with open cockpits in tandem. unlike the *Transatlantic* of 1919 which had a closed cabin and seats together in echelon. Like the 1919 long-range machine both wings were extended by a full extra bay giving a span

Coutinho and Cabral with Santos Dumont.
(Naval Museum, Lisbon)

The 'Lusitania' coming down at St. Peter and Paul Rocks.
(Naval Museum, Lisbon)

The end of the 'Lusitania' at St. Peter and Paul Rocks in mid-Atlantic. (Naval Museum, Lisbon)

of 62 ft as compared with the 46 ft 1 in. span of the standard IIID. Larger floats were fitted to bear the load and carry extra fuel, the total carried being 330 gallons giving a expected endurance of rather over 18 hours, whereas the standard IIID carried only 105 gallons. The all-up weight of the 'Transatlantic Load Carrier' as Fairey's called it was thus increased from 5050 lb to 7250 lb. This is thought to have been a record for a single-engined aircraft at that date. F400 was built in four months and first flew on 4 January 1922; it was then sent to Portugal by ship and reassembled under Fairey supervision. It was named *Lusitania,* the Roman name for Portugal.

As all three Fairey seaplanes were eventually used in completing the flight to Brazil, it seems appropriate to mention the others here also. Most accounts, if they mention the back-up planes at all, merely state that they were ordinary IIID's with some limited extra tankage added. This is true of F402, the *Santa Cruz,* which completed the flight and stands to this day in the Maritime Museum in Lisbon for all to see.

On the other hand, photographs show that F401 was certainly not a standard IIID and it appears to have been prepared as a special back-up plane for the *Lusitania.* It differed from F400 and F402 in that it had wings of unequal span, like the empennage of the earlier Fairey IIIB.

The three Fairey seaplanes were ready in Portugal in January 1922, which gave little enough time for flight testing if, as they hoped, the aviators were to leave in March to get the best possible weather.

As the *Lusitania* could only carry two and Coutinho, who was dead keen to go on the flight, was not a qualified pilot, he went over to England in the latter part of 1921 to train extensively on Fairey aircraft at Southampton. Dual control was fitted to the *Lusitania* so that Cabral could get some rest as the stages envisaged for this rather slow seaplane would run up to ten, eleven or even more hours. The strain of the voyage was expected to be considerable and the responsibility of the navigator no less than that of the pilot if some of the small island targets were to be found. The pair seemed rather mature men for this sort of adventure as Cabral was nearly 41 and Coutinho 53.

The Portuguese Government besides putting up the cash for the special seaplane also ordered three warships to support the attempt. The first was the 1250-ton escort vessel *Republica* (ex-HMS *Gladiolus)* one of the Flower-class sloops built on the Clyde for the Royal Navy in 1915 under the Emergency War Programme. Another of these, HMS *Chrysanthemum,* is moored in the Thames. Second was the very lightly armed Despatch Vessel *5 de Outubro* of 1340 tons, built at Leith in 1900, and third the gunboat *Bengo* of 460 tons, built in Lisbon in 1917.

The *Republica* which carried fuel, spares and engineering staff for the aircraft was ordered direct to the Cape Verde Islands and thence to the Brazilian island of Fernando Noronha, some 300 nautical miles off the Brazilian mainland. The other two ships proceeded to Las Palmas in the Canary Islands and, after seeing the aviators arrive, one ship steamed on to Cape Verde and the other returned to Lisbon. The three ships left Lisbon on 25 March. All was then ready for the flight by 30 March, wind and weather permitting. As a warm gesture from the Government both aviators received a step in promotion 'por distincão', Sacadura Cabral to Commander and Gago Coutinho to Rear Admiral.

So on that morning, with a light favourable wind, the *Lusitania* took off from the Tagus at 07.00 GMT for the Canaries and Las Palmas. After an uneventful flight of seven and a quarter hours land was sighted, vindicating the navigation of the new Admiral, out of sight of a landmark for nearly seven hours. Touching down at 15.37 GMT at Las Palmas the 703 nautical miles had been completed in 8

The second Fairey seaplane used in the crossing, also lost at sea.
(Naval Museum, Lisbon)

hours 37 minutes — so far so good. For this stage only 220 gallons of petrol were carried and *Lusitania* took off easily in 15 seconds.

Some problems had arisen on this leg of the flight; two bracing wires were broken on touching down, which was not serious, and water got into the floats, which was; for unless there were facilities for pulling the aircraft ashore and emptying the floats completely before flight it might not be possible to get enough fuel on board for the expected stage of 1260 nautical miles from the Cape Verde Islands to Fernando Noronha. They noticed also on the first stage that petrol consumption was higher than tests had shown in Britain or Lisbon.

On 2 April Cabral moved the *Lusitania* from Las Palmas to the Bay of Gando 15 miles away to get a better take-off and on 5 April they accomplished without difficulty their next main stage, the 850 nautical miles to São Vicente in the Cape Verde Islands; this took 10 hours 43 minutes at an average speed of 79.5 knots. On this leg the rather grim fact was confirmed that the *Lusitania* was using 20 gallons an hour instead of the estimated 18 and that full tanks of 330 gallons would therefore only last 16 hours, which meant that the stage from the Cape Verde Islands to Fernando Noronha would have to be accomplished at an average speed of 80 knots with no reserve. This required favourable conditions of wind all the way and floats emptied of water at the start; hardly a fair risk. Their choice then was either to call the whole attempt off or to take petrol from their escort vessel at sea at a rendezvous at the Rocks of St. Peter and Paul, virtually in the open Atlantic, which would cut down the non-stop stage to 908 nautical miles. The idea of calling the expedition off was one which they could not accept as great enthusiasm for their flight was already abroad. So the harsh decision to aim for the Rocks of St. Peter and Paul was taken and the *Republica* was ordered to leave for the rendezvous there.

It had been thought that the navigational task of finding Fernando Noronha, a mountainous volcanic island about 10 km square, would be difficult enough but nothing like the difficulty of finding the uninhabited Rocks of St. Peter and Paul which were only 650 feet across and a few feet above the water, a formidable target to hit after nearly 1000 statute miles in the open cockpit of a slow biplane with no radio.

To cut down the non-stop distance to a minimum the *Lusitania* after some days waiting for weather left São Vicente, the capital of Cape Verde Islands, on 17 April and flew to Porto Praia on the island of São Tiago, 170 nautical miles which was accomplished in $2\frac{1}{4}$ hours. Next day they took off at the third attempt on their hazardous flight to meet the *Republica* at the Rocks of St. Peter and Paul.

Cabral had calculated that if he took on board 255 gallons of petrol he could fly for 12 hours, which would require a rather higher average speed than could be obtained without a favourable wind if he was to reach the Rocks. A helping wind was to be expected but they found to their dismay after two hours that they had consumed no less than 60 gallons, a high figure probably caused by evaporation. An hour later they were 650 nautical miles short of their destination and they could count on eight hours' petrol at 20 gallons an hour. Cabral and Coutinho had to face the disagreeable fact that they needed a speed of over 80 knots for eight hours to make it at a time when their speed was only 72. They had to decide whether to put back but chose to carry on wondering every minute of the next eight hours whether their engine would die from lack of fuel.

Fortune favoured the brave and the helping wind freshened and pushed their speed up to 80 knots. At 14.30 they crossed the Equator and at 16.00 hours their main tanks were empty leaving them 24 gallons in the gravity tank, enough for about an hour and a quarter more. But at 17.00 the almost miraculous navigation of the old

The third Fairey seaplane, the 'Santa Cruz', used in the crossing leaving Fernando Noronha.
(Naval Museum, Lisbon)

Admiral — for eleven hours out of sight of land — showed them the Rocks of St. Peter and Paul dead ahead and the *Republica* a few miles to the north-west. At 17.15 Cabral cut the motor to come down alongside the ship. He had less than a gallon left in his tank.

Unfortunately the sea was rougher than was hoped and neither the Rocks nor the *Republica* offered any real shelter. In coming down one of the floats was damaged. Water came in fast and after this most notable flight the *Lusitania* had to be abandoned and went below the Atlantic to join her maritime namesake. The flight had lasted 11 hours and 21 minutes and for the first time Portugal and Brazil had been joined by air.

No doubt exasperated and depressed by the loss of their aircraft Coutinho and Cabral were nevertheless the subject of world interest and approval.

Flight pontificated thus:

> 'Most of the world's long-distance flights have been made by British crews in British machines engined by British power plants, and it would have been desirable that in this instance also the daring adventures (sic) should have been of our race. However, both officers are of a nation which has been for centuries our ally and with which we still have the very closest relations and we can therefore view without jealousy their splendid achievement'.

In an earlier issue *Flight* had said that their achievement was 'a very fine performance indeed and deserves to rank among the historical flights of the world'.

The Aeroplane as usual was rather more to the point; they said:

> 'The last stage — of just on 1000 miles terminating on a group of rocks whose total area is about 20 acres with no other land within 200 miles or more — must be regarded as an extremely fine piece of accurate navigation, particularly considering the very great strain necessarily imposed by something about 12 hours' continuous flying, all of it within the tropics'.

The Portuguese Government decided at once to send out their back-up plane, F401, and the aviators intended to resume their flight from the Rocks so as to cover the whole flight plan, when the new Fairey arrived. The *Republica* steamed with Coutinho and Cabral to Fernando Noronha to await orders and made a short visit to the mainland. The Lloyd Brasileiro offered to transport the new plane on SS *Bagé* and it was put on board in Lisbon.

On 4 May the *Republica* with the airmen aboard set out to make a rendezvous with the *Bagé* at the St. Peter and Paul Rocks which took place on 6 May. A lighter sea made it possible to leave a plaque on the Rocks recording the flight of the *Lusitania* but it was still considered too rough to risk putting the new plane on to the water. As the *Bagé* had passengers aboard they could not hang about for fair weather so both ships and F401 continued on to Fernando Noronha where the aircraft was put onto the water on 8 May.

In order to cover the stretch between Fernando Noronha and the Rocks and not leave any of the ocean unflown the aviators had to start, as it were, at the wrong end. Not wishing to risk another descent in the open sea, Cabral decided to make a flight from Fernando Noronha as far as the Rocks, circle them and fly back to base non-stop, a distance of 650 nautical miles. An extra fuel tank was fitted, to put the petrol capacity up to 161 gallons and the range to 670 nautical miles, which seemed enough.

On 11 May they took off at 09.00 local time and at 1.30 pm they were in sight of the Rocks and ready to turn for home. By 3.25 pm they switched tanks and were left with 50 gallons to make it back to base which they could have expected to reach in rather over two hours.

However at this point the motor began to cut out and a few minutes later at 3.35 pm stopped altogether, no doubt from a fuel blockage from dirt in the new tank. They climbed on to the floats, took stock of the position and found it disagreeable, the engine silent, 170 nautical miles from home, and about 30 miles west of the

The Fairey IIID 'Santa Cruz' which completed the first crossing of the South Atlantic.
(Naval Museum, Lisbon)

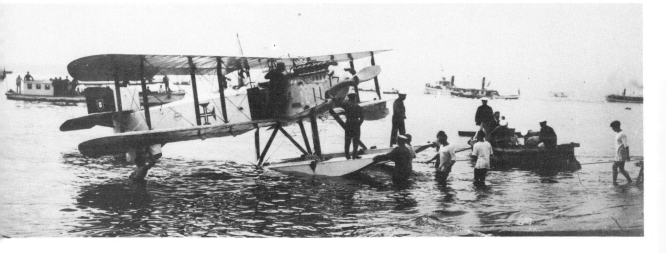

Jubilant Admiral, Gago Coutinho, at Rio de Janeiro. (Naval Museum, Lisbon)

main shipping lane; the *Republica* by plan was 100 nautical miles from them and could not be expected to reach them before 1 am. Luckily the wind was light, easterly. They made attempts to start the engine, succeeded once and got some action from it but it failed again permanently at 10.25 pm. By this time the tail of the plane was breaking up under the buffeting of the waves and it seemed that the Fairey would not hold together much longer. Just before the midnight they saw the lights of a ship and fired three Verey lights. Three-quarters of an hour later they were alongside the British cargo ship *Paris City* (Capt. A. E. Tamlyn) in passage from Cardiff to Rio de Janeiro. The ship had picked up a radio message about 10 pm that a plane was in trouble between the St. Peter and Paul Rocks and Fernando Noronha, altered course and found it. Next morning, 12 May, the plane was seen to be in bad shape with the floats submerged. The *Republica* had arrived at 6.30 am but the plane was too damaged to be towed and could not be hauled aboard, so they had to be content with saving the engine and the instruments and allowing the second Fairey to join its sister below the Atlantic.

Immediately public support arose in Portugal and Brazil by way of subscriptions and general clamour and the Portuguese Government were ready to chance their last seaplane. The standard Fairey IIID[1], F402, now named *Santa Cruz* was made ready and shipped on the cruiser *Carvalho Araújo,* which reached Fernando Noronha on 2 June. The aircraft, which arrived in good shape, had the normal tanks of 102 gallons plus an extra, carrying 35 gallons; these were expected to give an endurance of $7\frac{1}{2}$ hours, ample for the flights that remained.

[1] The public subscription enabled the Government to buy another IIID, No. F411, and later seven more were obtained.

*Sacadura Cabral and Gago
Coutinho.*
(Naval Museum, Lisbon)

By the morning of 5 June all was ready, by 8.48 am they were airborne and by 8.55 they were en route for Recife (Pernambuco) and the mainland of Brazil. They sighted the coastline before midday and at 13.20 they put down in the port of Recife. That was the last huge step, the completion of the crossing of the South Atlantic. After that it was all downhill — Bahia on 9 June, Porto Seguro on the 13th, Vitória on the 15th and on 17 June Rio at last, and a wild tumultuous welcome. Amid the thousands of congratulations there was a telegram from King George V. As *Flight* said, 'Our old allies, ever good navigators at sea, now equally good in the air'.

Although this journey had lasted for 80 days and used three aircraft it was long before it was bettered. The log read:

Stage	Date	Nautical miles	Time
Lisbon - Las Palmas	30 March	703	8hr. 37m.
Las Palmas - Gando	2 April	15	21m.
Gando - S. Vicente	5 April	849	10hr. 43m.
S. Vicente - S. Tiago	17 April	170	2hr. 15m.
S. Tiago - Rocks	18 April	908	11hr. 21m.
F. Noronha - Rocks - Sea	11 May	480	6hr. 34m.
F. Noronha - Recife	5 June	300	4hr. 32m.
Recife - Bahia	8 June	380	5hr. 30m.
Bahia - P. Seguro	13 June	212	4hr. 03m.
P. Seguro - Vitória	15 June	260	3hr. 40m.
Vitória - Rio de Janeiro	17 June	250	4hr. 50ms

		Nautical miles	Time
Total flying distance and time:		4527	62hr. 26m.
Deducting flight from Rocks to coming down on the way back to F. Noronha:		160	2hr. 12m.
Total distance and time for passage Lisbon - Rio		4367	60hr. 14m.
Average speed: 72.5 knots			

According to Admiral Ricou, the head of the Portuguese Maritime Museum, it was Cabral who was the moving spirit of the flight but because of his early death the renown for the first South Atlantic crossing settled on the head of Admiral Gago Coutinho who lived to the ripe age of 90 and died in 1969.

Cabral left the Navy in 1924 in order to attempt a flight around the world in a Fokker single-engined monoplane with floats. His intended route was from Lisbon to Macau, the Portuguese colony in

Parade of Atlantic fliers in Rome, 1932, with Sir Arthur Whitten Brown, General Balbo and Gago Coutinho in the front line.
(Naval Museum, Lisbon)

China, then to Yokohama and finally to St. John's, Newfoundland, and via the Azores to Lisbon, a total distance of 19,500 miles with engine changes at Rangoon and Vancouver. However, it was not to be; he left Holland in his seaplane on 15 November 1924 to fly to Portugal and was never seen again.

8.
Round the Top of the World

Arthur Brisbane, the famous American newspaper editor and pundit, wrote: 'History will for ever record, if only in two lines, the dates and names connected with the first human flight around the world'. Well yes, the names are in the record books but somehow Smith and Arnold, Nelson and Harding do not seem to be so lodged in memory as the less organised and often less successful aviators of the years between the wars.

A flight around the world involving a transatlantic stage and a passage of some part of the Pacific, even up at the 'shallow end' near the Bering Strait, was a formidable prospect in 1923 but, as with the conquest of the North Atlantic by the United States Navy, so the mustering of a highly detailed, organised and expensive operation by the American Army succeeded — at a slow, methodical pace, with depots and dumps all around the world, 480 items at each depot, and an Advance Officer in charge of each. Special aircraft were designed and built, spare engines were in readiness on the route, propellers and wheels and floats to enable the aircraft to be appropriately shod for the various stages. Where the flights were over stretches of water, the US Navy had ships on duty. The consent of 22 governments had to be obtained.

The first suggestion of an around-the-world flight was made in 1914 when the sponsors of the Panama Exhibition in San Francisco — which was to be held in 1915 to celebrate the opening of the Panama Canal — proposed to organise a race around the world for aeroplanes. The time limit was to be 90 days and the route to be followed was from San Francisco to New York, Belle Isle (Newfoundland), Cape Farewell (Greenland), Iceland, Stornoway, Edinburgh, London, Paris, Berlin, Warsaw, St. Petersburg, Moscow, Tobolsk, Tomsk, Irkutsk, Vladivostok, Korea, Japan, Kamchatka, the Bering Straits and Alaska and so back to San Francisco. The war in Europe put a stop to this venture which, although it had been sanctioned by the Aero Club of America, would have proved more hazardous than the famous motor race from New York across Siberia to Paris in 1908.

The next attempt at a flight around the world was planned by the Vickers organisation in 1922, with the success of Alcock and Brown across the Atlantic and of Sir Ross and Sir Keith Smith to Australia already to their credit. The two brothers Smith were intending to fly eastwards in a Vickers Viking amphibian with a single 450 hp Napier Lion engine starting on 25 April 1922. Their route was intended to be: Croydon, Lyons, Rome, Athens, Cairo, Baghdad, Basra, Karachi, Calcutta, Mandalay, Hanoi, Hong Kong, Shanghai, Fusan, Tokyo, Kashira, Petropavlovsk, Attu, Dutch Harbor, Kodiak, Yakutat, Wrangell, Vancouver, High River, Winnipeg, Borden, New York, Sydney (Nova Scotia), St. John's and over the Atlantic. Unfortunately Sir Ross Smith and Lt. Bennett were killed on 13 April at Brooklands when their aircraft spun into the ground from 1200 ft.

The challenge was then taken up by another British team, Capt. Norman Macmillan, Major W. T. Blake and Lt. Col. L. E. Broome, sponsored by the *Daily News*. They obtained the use of four aircraft from the Aircraft Disposals Company, two DH9 three-seaters, with Siddeley Puma engines, for the stages to Calcutta and across America, a Fairey IIIC float plane for the stage from Calcutta to Vancouver and a Felixstowe F3 flying boat for the last stage across the Atlantic via Greenland, Iceland and the Faeroes. Macmillan's expedition, with cinematographer G. H. Malins replacing Broome, left London on 25 May 1922 in one of the DH9s. The flight was beset by troubles from the start and only reached Calcutta in August with Blake ill with appendicitis. Macmillan and Malins decided to go on alone and after only a 15-minute test flight of the Fairey they left

The take-off from San Diego, California. (Smithsonian Institution)

Calcutta for Akyab across the Bay of Bengal on 19 August. They had engine trouble, had to come down in a rough sea to clear it, restarted and while taxying to the Island of Lakhidia ran aground on a mudbank. They got away after being stranded for two days and three nights and made for Chittagong. Again the engine failed and they had to descend and they taxied with a waterlogged float towards land. Their fuel ran out, the plane heeled over backwards and finally got lodged on a mudbank where Macmillan and Malins spent another 24 hours before being rescued on 24 August. So ended that attempt.

In 1923 there were no around-the-world essays but the announcement was made that year by Major General Patrick, Chief of the US Army Air Service, of their planned flight for 1924. Five efforts to outstrip the Americans were made in 1924, none of them successful, and two more might have been attempted that year — by Cabral from Portugal in the Fokker seaplane in which he lost his life and by McIntosh and Tymms of Great Britain in the special Fairey Fremantle seaplane if it had been ready in time.

The first attempt to forestall the USA was by the British team of Squadron Leader MacLaren, Flt. Lt. Plenderleith and Flt. Sgt. Andrews in a Vickers Vulture amphibian with a single Napier Lion engine of 450 hp which left Calshot on 15 March 1924 before the American squadron had started from California. This flight was sustained by Vickers, Napiers and oil company interests.

MacLaren's flight, which had had spare engines awaiting them in Tokyo and Toronto, left via Le Havre, Lyons, Civita Vecchia, Rome, where they had troubles, Brindisi and Corfu where they made a forced landing; a new engine was fitted and they went on via Athens, Cairo, Ziza (Amman), Baghdad, Basra, Bushire and reached Bundar Abbas on the Persian Gulf on 23 April. Continuing via Chahbar and Karachi they had a forced landing in Parlu. Needing a new engine which apparently could only come by boat, they pressed on with a temporary engine from Baghdad via Nasirabad and Bamraoli to Calcutta where the proper new engine was fitted.

No. 4 at Unalaska, Alaska.
(Smithsonian Institution)

One of the survivors at Kirkwall in the Orkneys. (BBC/Hulton)

Leaving Calcutta, they crashed at Akyab on 24 May near where Macmillan and Malins had come to grief; the crash was attributed to waterlogging of the plane in torrential monsoon rains. The American ground staffs who were servicing their own around-the-world fliers in Tokyo were most sympathetic and helpful whereas our own naval commanders in the Far East apparently were not.

The US destroyer *John Paul Jones* brought a new machine from Tokyo to Hong Kong in crates. There the crates were transferred to another US destroyer *William B. Preston* and taken to Akyab, arriving on 11 June. Friendship for a rival could not have gone further. MacLaren and his team were hoping to meet the American fliers at some spot and their paths crossed on 25 June between Akyab and Rangoon. MacLaren and his crew, who were sheltering from a storm in a bay on the Burma coast, saw the three American planes fly over westwards through the rain without themselves being seen. MacLaren's amphibian continued on through Kyaing Creek, Rangoon, Tavoy, Bangkok, Vinh and Haiphong which they reached on 30 June. Thence to Hong Kong, Foochow, Shanghai, Kagoshima, Susami, Yandoon, Tokyo, Minata, Kushiro, Yetorofu Is., Urup, Petropavlovsk in Kamchatka. They ended by crashing while attempting the stage to Attu in the Aleutian Islands, near Nikolski on Komandorski Island on 1 August.

So ended MacLaren's fine effort in the treacherous weather of the North Pacific, an area which the successful American team also found inhospitable. According to the *US Aircraft* yearbook for 1925:

'MacLaren's effort was a splendid sporting attempt. His organisation and supply arrangements were necessarily inadequate. That he got as far as he did was

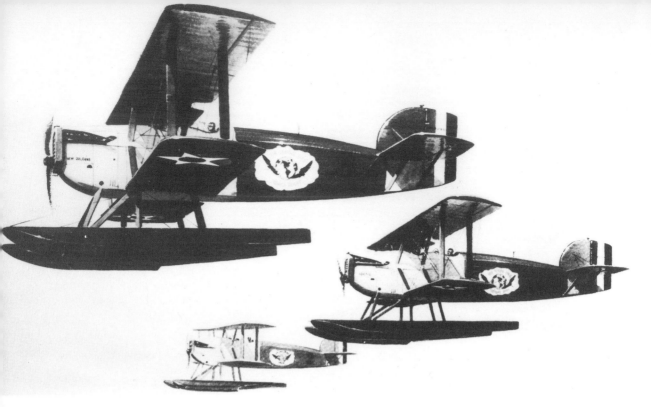

Three planes together in flight.
(Real Photo/Ian Allan)

regarded as remarkable under the circumstances. He was trapped in a dense fog while attempting to fly from Petropavlovsk Kamchatka, to Nikolski in the Komandorski Islands of the North Pacific and upon landing near the shores of Behring Island his plane was hopelessly damaged. An American destroyer hastened to his assistance with an extra plane (from Japan) but the season was then too far advanced to merit continuance across the rigorous stretches of the lower Arctic.'

Next away — and before the US Army took off — was the Portuguese team of Brito Pais and Sarmento de Beires who left Lisbon in a Breguet XVIB2 biplane on 2 April to fly first to the Portuguese colony of Macau in South China and if all was going well to fly on around the world. However their aircraft, which had been provided by public subscription, was wrecked at Macau so having flown 11,000 miles in twenty-three stages they called it a day.

The next hare to try to beat the Americans was the extrovert roly-poly French pilot Lieut. Peletier D'Oisy, nicknamed Pirolo 'à la bonne figure ronde', who left Paris on 24 April 1924 with Sgt. Vesin in a standard Breguet XIXA2 sesquiplane with a 400 hp Lorraine Dietrich engine. The Breguet XIX family with its large parasol upper wing and its short stubby lower wing was famous in the twenties and many feats and records were achieved by it. 'Pirolo' made a headlong flight aiming first at Tokyo with around-the-world continuation in mind. By 29 April he was in Karachi travelling from Paris via Bucharest, Adrianople, Constantinople, Konin, Aleppo, Baghdad, Basra, Bushire and Bundar Abbas, and in twelve days he was in Calcutta with a stop at Agra. Charging on via Rangoon, Bangkok, Saigon, Hanoi and Canton Peletier D'Oisy finally came to grief on 20 May when his plane was bunkered and wrecked at the 13th hole on the Kiangwan golf course in Shanghai, in a hazard which was also a drainage ditch for the race course that shared the site. The flight of 9200 miles had so far been spectacular but the continuation of it in a slower machine via Pekin, Peitaho, Mukden, Pyong Yang, Hiroshima and Osaka to Tokyo was listless by comparison and the around-the-world attempt was called off.

So the way looked clear for the Americans to continue their deliberate planned attempt to full success. The US Army started by ordering an experimental aircraft from the infant Douglas company

The four planes over Sitka, Alaska.
(U.S. National Archives)

of Santa Monica, California, of which more was to be heard in later years. This was a two-seater biplane with a span of 50 ft driven by a single 450 hp Liberty engine; with 465 gallons of petrol the all-up weight was four short tons. They had detachable undercarriages so that they could operate as seaplanes or land-planes. After stringent testing of the prototype, four of the Douglas Cruisers were ordered together with a spare machine, and the pilots and mechanics who were to make the attempt went to watch the building of their own planes.

The Douglas machines were ready early in March 1924. Three of them were then flown to Seattle between 17 and 21 March and the fourth left two days later to catch up. In Seattle the aeroplanes were named after four US cities with libations of suitable water. The squadron then was:-

'Seattle' (flagship)	'Chicago'	'Boston'	'New Orleans'
Major Martin	Lt. Smith	Lt. Wade	Lt. Nelson
Sgt. Harvey	Lt. Arnold[1]	Sgt. Ogden	Lt. Harding

All the pilots were fully experienced men with service dating from America's entry into World War I and the sergeant mechanics were highly skilled men chosen by examination. During the course of the

[1]Sgt. Turner had been named but was rejected for health reasons.

flight the distinctions, made in those days, between commissioned and non-commissioned officers were embarrassing and Ogden was promoted to second-lieutenant when they reached Japan.

The advance planning had been meticulous and there is little doubt that Lts. Brown and Streett, who were responsible, contributed greatly to the success of the flight. So too did Lt. Nelson, who was engineering officer of the squadron as well as pilot of the *New Orleans;* in Grover Loening's view he was the real hero of the expedition.

On 6 April the four US World Cruisers left Seattle, the official starting point, rigged as seaplanes — the form in which they were to fly to Calcutta. The planners had elected to fly east to west, contrary to all other world attempts and contrary to the prevailing winds. The reasons given for this were that the weather was likely to be more favourable by this route at their estimated times although the monsoon over Asia could be expected. No doubt the thought of a triumphant tour of the United States from Boston, the intended place of arrival, was in mind. The aircraft carried shotguns and fishing tackle and each man had a pistol as well as Very pistols. They carried concentrated food, first aid kits, canvas message bags, some spares, a 60lb ships's anchor and 50 ft of rope, but neither parachutes nor life-jackets. There was a limit of 300 lb on what was carried for the planes could not get off the water if they weighed more than 8200 lb. In the hotter parts of the earth this proved very difficult and unnecessary gear was unloaded *en route.*

The first division of the flight was intended to be from Seattle to Chicagoff on Attu Island, the most westerly of the Aleutian Islands, a distance of 3250 statute miles, in seven stages planned as follows:

		Distance (miles)	Date of Arrival
Seattle -	Prince Rupert	610	6 April
	Sitka	300	10 April
	Seward	610	14 April
	Chignik	450	15 April
	Dutch Harbor	400	19 April
	Atka Is. (Nazan)	350	3 May
	Attu Is. (Chicagoff)	530	9 May
		3250	

The Advance Officer was Lt. Clayton Bissell based on Dutch Harbor in the Aleutians.

Major Martin, the commanding officer, with Sgt. Harvey was in trouble all through this stage, breaking a strut and some wires in landing at Prince Rupert, and they were then forced down off Cape Igrak with a hole in the crankcase and a ruined engine on 14 April. Next day after spending over twelve hours in the plane they were rescued by the destroyer *Hull* and towed to the shore settlement of Kanatak where they awaited a new engine from their Dutch Harbor base; this was fitted and Martin and Harvey got away on 25 April and after the usual gales and snowstorms and a pause in shelter for weather they arrived at Chignik, by which time the other three planes had gone on ahead to Dutch Harbor, the main base for Division One. After being weatherbound at Chignik, Martin and Harvey finally took off to try to catch the others up on 30 April but they got off course and crashed in the wild uninhabited mountains of the Alaskan peninsula in the usual thick and freezing weather.

Luckily they escaped serious hurt although the *Seattle* was wrecked. After sleeping the night on board they awoke to fog and stayed another 24 hours where they were, rather than risk being lost in the mountains or falling down a precipice. On 2 May they decided in spite of fog to try to get down to the coast. Crossing two mountain ranges they set out to follow a creek down to the sea but realising that it would lead them to the Bering Sea side of the peninsula, which was unlikely to be inhabited, they returned to the plane on 3 May. There they made some sort of encampment, kept a fire going, ate their iron rations and later on shot a couple of ptarmigan with an Army pistol. Both men suffered intermittently from snow blindness. They set out again on 4 May and followed a stream towards a lake they had seen through their glasses, but had to sleep out. Struggling on, they had to sleep out for a second night but on 6 May they reached the lake on the shores of which was a hut with a cache of food and a stove. This stroke of luck enabled them to sit out a two-day snowstorm in relative comfort, warm up to a point, tolerably fed with the stores in the hut supplemented by ducks and rabbits which they shot. They discovered that they were at Lake Moller and twenty-five miles from Port Moller on the north side of the peninsula. After a reconnaissance they set out to walk 25 miles to the Port Moller cannery on 10 May but were seen by a native boatman, Jake Oroloff, and picked up and returned to civilisation.

The squadron, battered by weather and reduced to three planes

The Vickers 'Vulture' for the MacLaren attempt to fly around the world, 1924. (Flight)

Major Martin and Sergeant Harvey who survived the wreck of the 'Seattle' in Alaska.
(U.S. National Archives)

by the loss of their leader, was put under the command of Lieut. Lowell Smith, who was ordered by the Chief of the US Air Service in Washington on 2 May not to wait for the missing men but to proceed with all speed to Japan. They had been at Dutch Harbor since 19 April so took off on 3 May for Atka Island along the Aleutian chain. After being weatherbound again they finally completed Division One at Chicagoff on Attu Island on 9 May. All the way from the start at Seattle the flight had to contend with bad weather, gales, rain, fog, snow, as they hugged the coast and dodged the peaks and promontories. There was no night flying but by day it was hazardous enough, always at low altitudes and often in fog or cloud; they were buffeted incessantly by strong winds and unpredictable violent squalls from the mountains called locally 'Willy-Wars'. It must have been a hideously uncomfortable trip for even when at rest in shelter they were often soaked through when working on the planes or refuelling. As a local resident at Dutch Harbor said to the journalist and author Lowell Thomas, 'We only have two seasons. This winter and next winter.'

The next stage of the around-the-world flight was the historic one, with the crossing of the Pacific and the Date Line on 15-16 May, for the first time in history by air, and the first flight from America to Asia. True, the distance necessary for this notable event was only 400 miles, the nearest point of Asia being the Russian Komandorski Islands for visiting for which no permission had been obtained. Nevertheless they came over the islands to dodge a storm and alighted in open but sheltered water near Nikolski the main port of the Komandorskis; the Russians were courteous but told them to

Three of the crews for the around the world flight. (U.S. National Archives)

clear out, which next day they did, reaching the Japanese Kurile Islands on 17 May.

Division Two was as follows:

		Distance (miles)	*Date of Arrival*
Attu Is. -	Komandorski Is.	400	16 May
	Paramashiru, Kurile Is.	427	17 May
	Hittokapu, Kurile Is.	500	19 May
	Minato, Japan	354	22 May
	Kasumiga Ura (Tokyo)	350	22 May
	Kashimoto	350	1 June
	Kagoshima	350	2 June
		2731	

The Advance Officer was Lt. Clifford Nutt based in Tokyo. Here the fliers were able to refit their aircraft after the vile weather they had suffered almost all the way from Seattle, so bad that in fact they had been going for 47 days which yielded only 80 hrs 24 min of flying time and were a month behind schedule. New floats, new engines and larger radiators were fitted in Japan and on 5 June they left Japan and were off on Division Three.

This was a major sector, covering the journey to Calcutta where the Advance Officer Lt. Lawson was based. The route was as follows:

		Distance (miles)	*Date of Arrival*
Kagoshima -	Shanghai	610	5 June
	Amoy	555	7 June
	Hong Kong	300	8 June
	Haiphong	500	10 June
	Tourane	395	11 June
	Saigon	530	16 June
	Kawrong Is.	340	18 June
	Bangkok	335	18 June
	Tavoy	240	20 June
	Rangoon	210	20 June
	Akyab	445	25 June
	Chittagong	180	26 June
	Calcutta	220	26 June
		4860	

The conditions on this division were less exacting and less arduous, though Smith and Arnold in *Chicago* had to come down off the Japanese coast and fit a new engine; they later wrecked this engine in central Indo-China making a forced landing in the jungle on a lagoon. A second new engine for the *Chicago* was brought overland from Saigon while the aircraft was towed by dug-out canoes to Tourane near Hue. By 20 June however all three planes were in Rangoon. Here Lowell had an attack of dysentery and the *New Orleans* was damaged by a collision with a river boat on the

Irrawaddy. So they did not reach Calcutta until 26 June, having flown over the British team of MacLaren *en route* the day before.

At Calcutta the World Cruisers were hauled out of the river and were serviced right in the centre of the city on the Maidan. New wings were fitted and the floats were replaced by wheels for the stage from India to England. Smith the leader had a fall and broke a rib but refused more than a minimum of delay, for the party had time to make up. The party indeed showed immense attention to duty when time and again they could have been swamped by hospitality. The risks of fatigue were serious with day-long flights and servicing the planes at the end of the day.

Leaving Calcutta the *Boston,* of all improbable things, carried a stowaway, Linton Wells, the Associated Press representative who could not bear to let them go, and he continued to ride as the third man all the way to Karachi; this was possible as the wheeled undercarriages weighed much less than the floats.

The Fourth Division of the flight under Lt. Halverson at Constantinople was as follows:

		Distance (miles)	Date of Arrival
Calcutta -	Allahabad	475	1 July
	Umballa	500	2 July
	Mooltan	325	3 July
	Karachi	475	4 July
	Chahbar	330	7 July
	Bundar Abbas	400	7 July
	Bushire	200	8 July
	Baghdad	275	8 July
	Aleppo	480	9 July
	Constantinople	600	10 July
		4060	

Karachi was a 'division point' on the fourth leg and here all the planes were fitted with fresh engines after only about 2000 miles.

Peletier d'Oisy's Breguet 'Jacqueline'. (Musée de l'Air)

*Another around the world
contender; a model of Brito Pais's
Breguet.*
(Musée de l'Air)

After Karachi the flight put on steam and so continued at a great
pace all the way to England, completing the two divisions from
Calcutta to Brough in Yorkshire in 17 days, catching up two weeks
of the month they had lost.

Charging on, the Fifth Division to London, whose Advance
Officer was Major Wash was soon completed, but not without
fatigue. Lowell Thomas's book[1] on the flight, which is an invaluable
source of information, reports that they fell asleep at the Folies
Bergère and when retiring for the night in a Paris hotel put this
notice on their bedroom doors: PLEASE DO NOT WAKE US
UNTIL NINE O'CLOCK TOMORROW MORNING UNLESS
THIS HOTEL IS ON FIRE; AND NOT EVEN THEN UNLESS
THE FIREMEN HAVE GIVEN UP ALL HOPE!!. The Stage Five
sped by thus:-

		Distance (miles)	Date of Arrival
Constantinople-	Bucarest	300	12 July
	Budapest	500	13 July
	Vienna	140	13 July
	Strasbourg	400	14 July
	Paris	250	14 July
	London	225	16 July
		1815	

[1]*The First World Flight,* by Lowell Thomas. Hutchinson 1925.

On 17 July they were in Brough on the Humber, preparing for the transatlantic leg at the Blackburn Aviation Company's works.

The aviators had a long spell at Brough, 13 days, as they had got ahead of their revised schedules and had to wait while the US Navy patrols and their own supplies got into position in Iceland and Greenland. The World Cruisers were refitted at Brough with floats and new engines with small radiators.

Before they left Brough on 30 July on the hardest and most exacting division of the whole enterprise two more teams were on around-the-world attempts with a faint hope of beating the Americans.

The more successful of these was an Argentine team consisting of Major Pedro Zanni of the Argentine Air Force with Lt. Nelson Page and Ch. Eng. Beltrane. They left Amsterdam on 22 July 1924 to fly eastwards around the world in a Fokker C IV seaplane with a Napier Lion engine. They reached Nasirabad on 2 August and Hanoi, where they crashed, on 18 August. With a new seaplane they pushed on as far as Tokyo and at that point turned it in.

Meanwhile the Italian team of Lt. Antonio Locatelli, Lt. V. Crossio, Engineer Lt. C. Marescalchi and navigator Lt. Rissili had left Pisa on 25 July in a twin-engined Dornier Wal (whale) flying boat of German design built under licence in Italy, to attempt to cross the Atlantic east to west for the first time by an aeroplane, flying via Marseille, Lausanne, Strasbourg, Rotterdam and Brough which they reached a day after the Americans had left.

Meanwhile the American team was in trouble. It had flown from Brough to Kirkwall in the Orkneys on 30 July and eventually, with the loss of the *Boston* at sea, the other two, *Chicago* and *New Orleans,* reached Hornafjord in Iceland. Out of Kirkwall the team, which usually flew together, had got separated in thick weather but Lt. Nelson and *New Orleans* got through to Iceland that first day, 2 August. *Chicago* and *Boston* feared that *New Orleans* was lost and started to look for it. Failing to find it, *Chicago* and *Boston* put back to Kirkwall. They left again on 3 August but just over an hour out, *Boston* (Wade and Ogden) had to put down onto the Atlantic with engine failure. *Chicago* was warned not to descend and went off to look for a rescue ship; they found the destroyer *Billingsby* north of the Faeroes and dropped message bags. After Wade and Ogden had been on the water for about five hours a trawler, the *Rugby-Ramsey,* found them and tried to tow. Within the hour the *Billingsby* and the four-funnelled cruiser *Richmond* came up. An attempt to hoist the *Boston* aboard failed and so did an attempt to dismantle the plane and haul the parts on board. Finally the plane capsized and sank under tow at 5.50 am on 4 August after 20,000 miles of travelling. Next day the two surviving planes flew on from Hornafjord to the more hospitable location of Reykjavik in Iceland, although they had to battle fierce gales on the way. In Reykjavik they had to put up with a maddening delay of 10 days as their Advance Officer, Lt. Le

Clair Schultze, was in difficulty organising supplies in Greenland, while the Advance Officer in Iceland, Lt. Crumrine, was trying to organise a weather service.

They had originally planned to fly from Iceland to Angmagssalik on the east coast of Greenland across open sea, about 500 miles, then follow the coast of Greenland around to Ivigtüt on the western side. The ice close inshore made this impossible so a new plan was made to fly over the sea for over 800 miles to Frederiksdal, around the tip of Greenland from Cape Farewell..

Meanwhile Locatelli and his Dornier had arrived in Iceland and it was agreed that he would fly in company with the Americans to Frederiksdal and use their services. They left Reykjavik together on the morning of 21 August but Locatelli was too fast to stay with them and pushed on ahead into bad weather. He decided to come down about 200 miles east of Cape Farewell and wait for the weather to mend. As almost always, a decision to alight on the open sea was disastrous; almost at once the sea began to pound his aircraft to pieces and hemmed in with pack ice he drifted helplessly for three days, unable even to taxi with his remaining engine. Immediately a systematic search for Locatelli was organised over an area of about 12,000 square miles by the American cruisers *Richmond* and *Raleigh.* By an almost inconceivable combination of skill and luck Locatelli and his crew were found about midnight on 24 August when a sharp-eyed lookout on the *Richmond* saw a brief gleam of light about 10 miles off. Under the flickering Northern Lights the crew of the Dornier was rescued but the flying boat had to be burned and sunk. As Locatelli afterwards said: 'This line (thrown from the ship) was like the first thread connecting us with life again'.

Smith and Arnold, Nelson and Harding, wisely chose to fight on through the storm which ruined Locatelli's flight and after an almost unbearably ugly battle with wind, fog and threatening icebergs, including one monster, they made it to Frederiksdal after

Lt. Antonio Locatelli who flew with the Americans and was later rescued by an American cruiser.
(Musée de l'Air)

Locatelli's Dornier 'Whale' flying-boat. (Smithsonian Institution)

the worst flight of the whole expedition, and at some ten hours, the longest. This constituted their Atlantic flight although mainland America was still to be reached. At their Greenland base at Ivigtüt they changed engines once more. In all the *New Orleans* used six engines between Seattle and Boston and *Chicago* used eight.

The Douglas 'Cruisers' left Greenland on 31 August and flew to Indian Harbor (Icy Tickle) in Labrador, during which flight *Chicago's* fuel pump motor failed and Arnold had to pump by hand for four hours. From there to Boston was no problem with stops at Hawkes Bay in Newfoundland, Pictou, Nova Scotia, where Wade and Ogden joined them in the new *Boston II* and at Casco Bay in Maine. In Lowell Thomas's report of this stage nothing is more memorable than the purchase of two dozen lobsters for a dollar in Pictou as the basis of a party.

So ended Division Six, which comprised these stages:

		Distance (miles)	Date of Arrival
London -	Brough	150	17 July
	Kirkwall	400	30 July
	Hornafjord	560	2 August
	Reykjavik	350	5 August
	Frederiksdal	825	21 August
	Ivigtüt	150	24 August
	Indian Harbor	572	31 August
	Hawkes Bay	350	2 September
	Pictou	420	3 September
	Casco Bay	400	5 September
	Boston	129	6 September
		4306	

The Advance Officers had been Lieutenants Crumrine, Schultze and Bissell.

Although the circumnavigation of the globe was not completed at Boston, the arrival here really marked the end of the world flight as the progress to Seattle took the form of a triumphal tour of the United States lasting three weeks. This was organised by Capt. Burdette White, and took in New York, Aberdeen, Washington, Dayton, Chicago, Omaha, St. Joseph, Muskogee, Dallas, Sweetwater, El Paso, Tucson, San Diego (with another engine change), Los Angeles, San Francisco, Eugene, Portland and finally ended at Seattle, on 28 September, 175 days and over 25,000 miles behind them since departure. Accounts vary for the distance flown but Lowell Thomas's record puts it at 26,345 miles by the two successful machines in 363 hours and 7 minutes of flying time, that is just over 15 days of flying out of 175 days.

C. G. Grey in *The Aeroplane* wrote:

> 'It was the Americans Wilbur and Orville Wright who were the first to fly an aeroplane under proper control. It was an American crew under Commander Read in a Curtiss-built flying boat who first flew the Atlantic. And it is in accord with precedent that an American team should be the first to circle the globe by air.
>
> What could be more natural? Such feats are achieved by grit, energy, pertinacity, determination, endurance and faith.
>
> Such human qualities, and especially faith in one's future, are precisely those which inspired the ancestors of these men to pull themselves up by the roots and press ever Westward to the promised land.
>
> Always the wave of conquest has flowed Westward and perhaps there is a significance in the fact that this flight should have encircled the earth in the direction in which all our ancestors have travelled'.

Congratulations were heaped upon the fliers — quite rightly; the President of the United States did them great honour and they were congratulated by messages from King George V and the Prince of Wales who was in USA.

Let Admiral Robinson of San Diego have the last word:

> 'Other men will fly around the earth but never again will anybody fly around it for the first time'.

Another around the world attempt was by Zanni's Fokker CIV.
(Musée de l'Air)

9.
Zeppelin Delivery

The Zeppelin Museum at Friedrichshafen is up four flights of stairs, but worth the effort for it shows the entire development of the rigid airship, one of the most interesting and compact chapters in the whole history of aviation, even if, as Kenneth Poolman tells us, 'was an aeronautical cul-de-sac[1]'. The big rigids, like the big ocean liners, were a thing apart, capable of growth up to an enormous size and even today there are those who believe that such giants, improved by modern knowledge, might yet have a part to play in transport. Barnes Wallis, the leading British airship designer of the 1930s, though more famous as the inventor of the bouncing bomb, did not share these views. When interviewed for the Transport Trust[2] and asked if he thought the airship might come back he replied: 'No, absolutely no, and I think these suggestions of the airship coming back are made by people who have no knowledge of the immense progress which we have made in heavier-than-air transport'.

In essentials these giants did not change much in the forty years of their existence — from the start with the ideas of one man, Count von Zeppelin, to the end with the disaster to No. 129 the *Hindenburg* and the subsequent breaking up of No. 127, the most famous and successful of all airships which bore his name.

The *idea* of a rigid airship was not new and one, the Schwarz airship, was actually built with thin metal cladding in 1897; it flew for a few moments before crashing. But the first thoughts, the painful experimentation and development — including the commitment of his entire fortune — and especially the driving determination needed to overcome innumerable troubles and setbacks which led to the successful production of the rigid airship, are all to the credit of one man Count Ferdinand von Zeppelin, and this too at an age when most men would have retired. He had able assistants, Kober the engineer, Müller-Breslau the theoretician and especially Dr Hugo Eckener; journalist, public relations man and later the most famous of airship captains, who in the early days 'came to scoff and remained to pray'.

Even when the technique of the large rigid airship was widely

[1]Kenneth Poolman in *Zeppelins over England,* (Evans Bros., 1960), quoting Dr Monk Gibbon.
[2]*Transport Pioneers of the 20th Century.* The Transport Trust, 1981.

known it seemed that only the Germans, and the Zeppelin Company at that, could make successful aircraft. In all, between 1900 and 1940 over 120 of these machines were built — over 100 of them during World War I — by the Zeppelin Company while only a handful, 22 were made, by the other German manufacturer Schütte-Lanz who used a wooden rather than a metal skeleton. France built only one, the *Spiess* in 1911-13, which had no success, while the three built by the United States the *Shenandoah,* the *Akron* and the *Macon,* in spite of access to German technology after the war, all came to grief by failing in the air in bad weather.

As described in Chapter 6, Britain laid down over the years twenty rigid airships though not all of these were built. With the notable exceptions of the Barnes Wallis designs, in part in the R9 and wholly in the R80 and the R100, we could only claim success with the R33 and R34 which meticulously copied the German L33.

LZ1 the first Zeppelin at Friedrichshafen, 1900.
(Zeppelin Museum)

It seems as if the German designers and the Zeppelin Company in particular had, apart from our Barnes Wallis, some monopoly of knowledge which escaped all imitators. The secret perhaps was no secret at all but only a thorough understanding of the stress relations of structures combined with aerodynamic knowledge. This for example the designers of our R101 seemed unaccountably to lack. If we had not been so dismayed by the loss of the R101 in 1930 it is possible that the R100, so intemperately broken up, might have had at least as useful a life as the German LZ126 or the even more famous LZ127, the *Graf Zeppelin.* It is possible too that the fiery loss of the LZ129, the *Hindenburg,* in 1937 — which may or may not have been sabotage — might have been averted if the distrust of Nazi Germany had not prevented use of the supply of

Fuel tanks inside the airship's envelope.
(Zeppelin Museum)

helium from the United States. At that time nothing in the air had a payload comparable to that of the big rigid airships; only when World War II was over did the capacity of the aeroplane, later accentuated by the jet engine, seal the fate of these huge unweildy and basically flimsy monsters. But for the time, for a few brief years around 1930, they seemed to hold the promise of a big future in air transport.

Count von Zeppelin was a Württemberger born at Konstanz on the lake of that name — the Bodensee — in 1838 before the Kingdoms of the German confederation were embraced by the German Empire in 1871. Like many young men of good family he chose the army as a career — the army of the King of Württemberg — and in this army he served on the side of Austria against Prussia in the Seven Weeks' War of 1866 and on the side of Prussia in the Franco-Prussian War of 1870-71.

In the army Zeppelin served with infantry, engineers and cavalry, had a university course at Tubingen and a visit to the United States in 1863 as an observer of the Civil War. He received a *laissez-passer* signed by President Lincoln to visit the Federal Armies and afterwards joined an expedition to explore the sources of the Mississippi.

He is said to have been blunt and outspoken and not to have suffered fools gladly and it is said that he hated England. If this is true the sentiment was by the end of his life cordially reciprocated. The Zeppelin raids on England in World War I aroused the deepest and bitterest feelings.

While in America Count von Zeppelin observed the use of balloons for military observations and went up in one at St. Paul,

Minnesota. He also took note of the use of balloons during the Siege of Paris. His interest in aviation, fired up by early French experiments with dirigible balloons and his own thinking, came into full play when he fell foul of the Prussian military establishment by his outspoken criticism of the Prussianisation of the upper ranks of the semi-independent royal armies of the German Empire. This reached the ears of the Supreme War Lord, Kaiser Wilhelm II, and Zeppelin's military career was finished. As a full Colonel he was noted as unfit for further command, promoted to Lieutenant General and at the age of 52 retired.

Zeppelin was then free to concentrate on his ideas for flying machines. The idea of a rigid framework of the new light metal aluminium, just becoming an article of commerce, separate bags of hydrogen inside the rigid carcase and an outside envelope over all looked a feasible prospect, especially now that internal-combustion engines were becoming available. It was clearly attractive to have a rigid frame, which would prevent the lamentable tendency of simple dirigible gasbags to sag or buckle, and so would permit a marked increase of size to be brought about to take advantage of the fact that a simple multiple of the linear dimensions would produce a cube effect in the volume and lifting power of the gasbag.

Zeppelin's first idea seems to have been 'a sort of articulated flying train' of separate gas-filled rigid units connected together by special couplings. At the front end was the 'locomotive unit' described in his patent of 1895 as 377 ft long with a diameter of 35 ft 6 in. with two Daimler engines of 11 hp; two separate tubular balloon trailers were attached, one to carry passengers and the other mail. It is probably just as well that this contraption never left the drawing board or that anyone was encouraged to embark on it.

By July 1900 a much more formidable aircraft had emerged from Count von Zeppelin's workshops; this was his first airship, the LZ1.

Handling the airship on the ground. (Zeppelin Museum)

Scraping together some money locally and with a considerable injection of his own capital he had built his first airship, a cigar-shaped unwieldy monster 420 ft long and 40 ft in diameter; it was gravely under-powered by two 15 hp Daimler engines. The fabric envelope contained 17 separate gasbags filled with hydrogen, fitted into a rigid frame of longitudinal girders and transverse rings, the whole braced by internal wires. This remained the basic principle of all future Zeppelins, for that is what they became known as. With time they became bigger, faster, more powerful and of better aerodynamic shape; cabins became enclosed and then absorbed into the framework. The first, the LZ1, had a volume of 400,000 cu ft, the last one to fly, the LZ130, which flew only a few test runs including a reconnaissance of the east coast of England just before World War II began, was a 7 million cu ft monster with 4400 hp in her engines.

LZ1 did not have a very happy start; it was too slow to fight a wind of more than 16 mph and with funds exhausted and the local backers dropping out this airship had to be discarded. Undismayed, Zeppelin started raising cash for a second airship and by November 1905 with the help of a lottery which the King of Württemberg had allowed him to organise, and with various grants and 400,000 marks of his own dwindling fortune, he had got his second machine in the air. With bigger engines of 65 hp LZ2 was a better ship than LZ1 but had a short life, being wrecked on her first flight in January 1906. This nearly finished the whole project but recovering from this setback Zeppelin again got together enough money, scraping together his last capital and profiting from another lottery, for a third try. The LZ3 first flew in October 1906 and was an unqualified success. This was the turning point; the army was suddenly interested, the Kaiser also. Government money appeared and the army ordered an airship if it came up to their specification. So a new airship the LZ4 was built; this was the biggest so far, over a half a million cu ft in volume with 105 hp Daimler engines. It flew very well and on a flight in July 1908 carried the King and Queen of Württemberg as passengers.

In August 1908 with a successful series of trial flights behind him Zeppelin set out to meet the army's requirements with a flight in LZ4 but just as success seemed within reach the airship, which had had to put down for engine repairs, was wrecked and burned on the ground in a sudden violent storm.

The publicity put about by Hugo Eckener, the young journalist after the old Count's last disaster suddenly caught on and from all over Germany money poured in, in large amounts and small, in admiration of Zeppelin's tough persistence. In all six million marks (about £300,000) came in which set the Zeppelin Company on its feet.

The army bought some airships but not enough for commercial success so Zeppelin with the aid of Eckener, now his enthusiastic supporter, reluctantly turned to commercial flying to provide work

Two U.S. rigid airships in their hangar.
(Illustrated London News)

for his new factory at Friedrichshafen. A subsidiary company, DELAG, was formed in November 1909 to operate charter and excursion flights between the principal German cities. The first passenger-carrying aircraft in the world, the LZ7, was ordered. She was completed in May 1910 and named *Deutschland* but had hardly got into her stride when she was wrecked. Eckener had now joined Delag as Director of Flight Operations, learned to fly and took command of the next ship the LZ8 or *Deutschland II* in February 1911; this airship too suffered storm damage in May of that year. The *Schwaben* came next in July 1911 and survived for nearly a year, carrying over 1500 passengers without mishap, before succumbing also to storm damage on the ground. Then between February 1912 and the outbreak of war Delag's three airships *Viktoria Luise* (LZ11), *Hansa* (LZ13) and *Sachsen* (LZ17) got into their stride and flew successfully with up to 20 passengers per trip making 1588 flights, covering 107,231 miles and conveying 10,197 people without accident.

Then came the war, the building of 100 Zeppelins, the bombardment of England instilling hatred and fear, naval reconnaissance and the final flaming hideous conquest of the airship by the aeroplane and the incendiary bullet. Count von Zeppelin died during the war on 8 March 1917.

When World War I ended the Zeppelin company, now nominally under the old Count's nephew Baron Gemmingen, hoped to restart commercial services around Europe, and to this end built two small airships the *Bodensee* (LZ120) and *Nordstern* (LZ114). The Allies,

US airship 'Los Angeles' moored to a warship. (Associated Newspapers)

however, would have none of this and both airships were seized for reparations, the *Bodensee* going to Italy and the *Nordstern* to France.

Things were then desperate for the Zeppelin Company but the Americans came to the rescue. Wishing to increase their naval fleet of airships and having only one rigid in service the ZR1 *Shenandoah* rebuilt from a captured German airship LZ96, they not unnaturally turned away from Britain as a builder after the disaster to their ZR2, which we called the R38, on test over the Humber and looked to Germany.

Unlike the other victorious Allies the Americans were willing to pay for a new Zeppelin, forgoing three million gold marks of reparations to do so. The clause of the peace treaty forbidding

Germany to build airships bigger than 1,100,000 cu ft was waived and the Zeppelin Company was allowed to build a ship up to the size of the biggest wartime Zeppelin, some two and a half million cu ft. So in June 1922 the contract for the US ZR3 (LZ126) was signed and the Zeppelin Company was back in business. As well as building the airship the company also contracted to deliver her to the United States and train the crews to serve in her.

The LZ126 was laid down early in 1922 and was completed in September 1924. She was the largest airship built to that date with a volume of 2,542,320 cu ft and five 350 hp Maybach engines for power. Top speed was supposed to be 80 mph. She turned out to be a fine ship with a long and useful life with the US Navy.

After a long run to Malmö and back after she was commissioned, Eckener and LZ126 were ready for the water jump. There were numerous delays but on Sunday 12 October — not on the 13th as several accounts state — Eckener and the LZ126 set out. Much was at stake on this voyage as Eckener was well aware, first the future of the Zeppelin Company and indeed the future of the airship, and secondly the highly desirable improvement in the relations of Germany with America to go with the hoped-for success of the German reconstruction loan about to be placed on the US market.

Eckener was escorted on board by detectives after a student had been arrested for making threats against him in protest at the airship being allowed to leave Germany as reparations. All through the last days before departure police and detectives had been active to prevent cranks and dissidents interfering with the flight and stowaways from getting on board.

Zeppelin LZ126 passing Basle en route to America. (BBC/Hulton)

At 6 am, garlanded with flowers, flying a large German flag, with a band pumping out 'Deutschland über Alles', the LZ126 was walked out of the shed at Friedrichshafen and shortly afterwards set out for the west.

Eckener had a crew of 27 on board with four American officers as guests[1]. The ship's company was as follows:

[1]See *Zeppelin and the USA* by Hans Knäusel. Luftschiffbau Zeppelin, 1976.

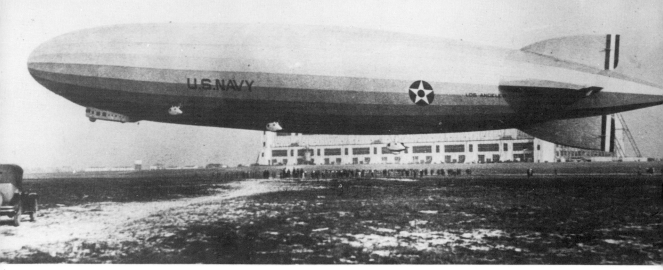

LZ126 transferred to the American flag and named 'Los Angeles'. (BBC/Hulton)

Commandant: H. Eckener

Watch Captains: E. H. Lehmann   H. C. Flemming

	Starboard Watch	Port Watch
Navigators	H. v. Schiller	A. Wittemann
Vertical steersman	M. Pruss	A. Sammt
Horizontal steersman	L. Marx	W. Scherz
Radio operators	W. Speck	L. Freund : H. Ladwig
Chief Engineer		W. Siegel
Balloon supervisor		L. Knorr
Engineer superintendent	Belser[1]	A. Grözinger
Engineers:		
Forward starboard gondola	A. Pfaff	A. Leichtle
Forward port gondola	A. Kiefer	W. Fischer
After starboard gondola	J. Auer	A. Thasler
After port gondola	K. Thielmann	Schwind
Rear gondola	M. Christ	E. Martin : E. Lang

American passengers:
Commander G. W. Steele
Lt. Cdr. J. H. Klein
Lt. Cdr. S. J. Kraus
Major G. Kennedy

Total: 31 persons

'Los Angeles' in an unusual posture.
(Smithsonian Institution)

Passing over Basle, Eckener set a slanting course across France, then over the mouth of Gironde to the Bay of Biscay, then over Spain leaving Europe behind at sunset. He was steering for the Azores and Bermuda and intended to make a southerly passage of the North Atlantic. They passed over Horta in the Azores at 2.35 pm on 13 October 1924.

From that point increasing head winds and bad weather changed Eckener's plans and he took the Zeppelin northward, making for Cape Sable at the foot of Nova Scotia. They were reported at midnight over Nova Scotia and saw the lights of Halifax. LZ126 passed Boston in the early hours of the morning of 15 October and

[1]In place of H. Pabst who had suffered a nervous breakdown owing to troubles with the starboard rear motor.

crowds turned out to cheer in spite of the hour. Over Mitchell Field on Long Island an escort of seven aeroplanes met her and she arrived over New York City at 7.50 am to the applause of the multitude. After an hour over the city the LZ126 headed for Lakehurst, N.J., the second airship in five years to reach the United States from Europe. With the aid of a ground crew of 350 she was down and moored in her hangar alongside the *Shenandoah* at 9.55 am (2.55 pm GMT). The wind had made the entry into the great shed difficult and the airship had to be walked all the way around the outside before the crew took it inside on the run. In all LZ126 had been in the air for 80 hours 45 minutes and flown 5006 miles.

President Coolidge sent a friendly message saying:

> 'It is a matter of great satisfaction to me and to the people of the United States that peaceful relations between Germany and America have been fully re-established, and that this great airship has inaugurated the first direct air flight between Germany and America'.

Later, on 25 October 1924, Mrs Coolidge named the airship, now the ZR3, *Los Angeles* as further evidence of her peaceful potential. She was emptied of hydrogen and helium from the ZR1 *Shenandoah* was transferred to her.

Eckener and his crew were fêted, had a ticker-tape parade up Broadway and brought about just what Eckener had hoped for, a rapprochement with the USA and a new lease of life for the Zeppelin Company, which went on from there to build the most famous of all airships, the next in line the LZ127 *Graf Zeppelin* and then later the ill-fated LZ129 *Hindenburg*.

The ZR3 had a useful if unexciting career with the US Navy — even if she once stood on her head at a mooring mast — exercising with the fleet, landing and tethering on aircraft carriers and fleet tenders, capturing and releasing small aeroplanes and making a number of long flights. In all she logged more than 5000 flying hours. She was withdrawn from service in June 1932 and only broken up in 1940, a sound, sensible and worthy ship.

10.
'Plus Ultra'

The three Franco brothers did well in the world. Nicolas the eldest prospered in diplomacy and business and ended up as Spanish Ambassador to Portugal; with a finger in many pies he became wealthy. The second brother Francisco, an Army man, became Generalissimo and the undisputed ruler of Spain after winning the Civil War of 1936-39, and so remained until he died in 1975.

The third brother, Ramón, a major in the Army Air Force, became a national hero by his flight across the South Atlantic to far Buenos Aires, long before his elder brothers had attracted any fame.

At that time, the early twenties, Spain was looking for opportunities in international aviation and the world was providing a huge arena in which to perform great feats so many of which captured the interest and imagination of nations and provided a nice profit as well.

Although Spain had stayed out of World War I and had emerged with some benefits she also had serious troubles. Poor parliamentary government, riots, assassinations, civil commotion, added to a difficult and nagging colonial war in Morocco, which had included one disastrous defeat, brought on the Primo de Rivera military dictatorship in 1923. A creditable or heroic performance was thus opportune.

The youngest Franco had been a military aviator in the Riff wars and by 1924 when he was 28 was thinking of an international long-distance flight which would put Spanish aviation on the map. The special relationship of language, sentiment, culture and shared history has always remained strong between Spain and her former colonial empire, not unlike the relationship between Britain and the United States, or Portugal and Brazil. It was not long before it became clear that the Argentine provided just the right destination for a spectacular world flight although the South Atlantic had already been crossed once, though laboriously, by the Portuguese. Spain, while not despising Cabral's and Coutinho's flight, was understandably inclined to regard it as little more than a lucky and courageous, indeed heroic, exploit and while a remarkable navigational exercise it had met with inordinate delays and the use of three unsuitable aircraft.

Franco's flying-boat and Columbus memorial in the south of Spain. (A.B.C.)

Ramón Franco wrote a paper setting out the proposal for a flight to the Argentine, after having learned that the Italian subsidiary of the Dornier Company[1] would provide a specially modified flying boat, a Dornier Wal (whale), at the same price as one of the standard flying boats which they were about to supply to the Spanish Air Force. Spain had no aviation industry at that time, although de la Cierva's autogiro was attracting interest, so that the use of a foreign machine was inevitable.

Franco's paper was well received by General Soriano, Director General of Aeronautics, who ordered that one of the four Dorniers being built for the government should be modified for the South American flight.

Franco originally chose Capt. Barberán as co-pilot and navigator but Barberán resigned from the Air Force as a result of a row with another squadron leader in North Africa in September 1925. Franco then took on 28-year-old Capt. Julio Ruiz de Alda as second pilot, navigator and wireless telegraphist. In addition Franco proposed to take with him his former soldier-mechanic from the Moroccan wars, 23-year-old Pablo Rada.

In October 1925, while their aircraft was still being finished, these three started strict physical training while supervising every detail of the completion of the plane at Pisa. A bargain was also made by Franco with the Spanish Minister of Marine to take with them a naval aviator, in return for the provision of ships to help on the flight. Admiral Cornejo appointed 25-year-old Lieut. Juan Durán, who was also a pilot, on the understanding that he would not be carried on the aircraft on the sector from the Cape Verde Islands to Fernando Noronha island off the Brazilian coast, that is the transatlantic crossing itself. A photographer, Leopoldo Alonso,

[1]The Germans at this period were not slow to get around the terms of the Treaty of Versailles. They were not allowed to build such aircraft as the Dornier 'Wal' so they set up an Italian subsidiary at Pisa to do so.

was also allowed to join the party on the same terms.

At this point another contender for the South Atlantic crossing by the same route appeared on the scene, an Italian major, the Marquis of Casagrande, who was reported as ready to take-off for Buenos Aires in a twin-hulled Savoia Marchetti S55 flying boat the *Alcione* (with two 500 hp Isotta-Fraschini engines) with Ranucci, Zachetto and Garello as crew. They left Lake Maggiore on 3 November 1925 and met Franco and his crew, who had left Pisa on 12 November, at the Spanish base of Los Alcazares. This permitted an exchange of views and data and left Franco with the impression that the Italians wouldn't bring if off; he said: 'I have talked with Casagrande and I am sure he will not make it. He is not prepared, he lacks data and knowledge'.

In this Franco was proved quite right. Casagrande reached Casablanca after a call at Gibraltar and a storm blew up which tore the Savoia from its moorings and wrecked it.

Undisturbed, Franco continued with his meticulous preparations so that in due time his Dornier could meet all his requirements: a speed of 185 kph at maximum load of 3300 kg; at 2500 kg load a speed of 195 kph; to be able to climb to 3000 metres with the lower load; and to stay at 500 metres above the sea with a load of 1500kg on one engine and make a figure of eight turn without losing height.

The Dornier 'Whale' flying boat was a highly successful long-lived type. Simple in essence, tough in performance, it fulfilled a number of functions in the twenties. Claudius Dornier, the designer, had worked for the Zeppelin company before the war and was put in charge of a flying boat subsidiary in 1914. His most famous aircraft — before his enormous 12-engined DoX flying boat of 1929 — was the Whale which first flew on 6 November 1922. Evading the Treaty of Versailles, the Germans farmed out the building of this aircraft to the Italian company Construzioni Meccaniche Aeronautiche SA, CMASA, which built about 150 of the total of some 300 built.

The plane comprised a sturdy tapering boat body, above which was a square-ended parasol wing hoisted above the boat's deck, on heavy struts. On top of the wing there were two engines back to back in tandem, the front engine driving a tractor propeller and the rear engine a pusher. There were stubby floats protruding from the boat body beneath the wing to improve stability when on the water and to add some lift in flight; the radiator was between the engines. There was a simple elevator and a simple rudder at the tail end of the boat and the wings were braced to the boat body by substantial struts. The design allowed a wide variety of engines to be used and many of those built had Rolls-Royce Eagle or Napier Lion engines. Franco chose Napier Lion engines of 450 hp for his 'Raid' as the Spanish called it.

The hull was built of duralumin which was also used for the centre section of the wing with varnished canvas on a duralumin frame on the outer sections. The total span was 22.5 metres and the overall length 16.25 metres. The maximum all-up weight was 6800 kg carrying 4000 litres of fuel, intended to give a 15-hour flight; it was even possible to carry petrol in drums on board the plane. This aircraft showed its versatility in being adaptable for civil as well as for the military uses and a number were built for use as small airliners. The body was divided into three compartments. Forward of the wing was a position in the nose for an observer behind which the two pilots sat with dual controls; there was a third space in this section for a radio operator and fuel tanks. The section under the wing held fuel tanks and space for one or two mechanics who could if necessary get out to the wing in flight, while the after section held the navigator and his equipment. Direction-finding radio was carried and used to great effect as well as normal navigational instruments.

Franco's flight aroused great public interest and outpourings of patriotism and national pride which captured the whole population. As General Gomá in his history of Spanish aviation (in translation) reports:

'It also awakened patriotic enthusiasm in every social class from which we can conclude that Franco's flight to America was for the man in the street the revelation that Spaniards could compete with the whole world in the most dangerous and difficult feats.

When the Spanish hydroplane landed in Buenos Aires many Spaniards cried and many were astounded, as if they had woken after a long sleep and were trying to find their place of origin . . .

There is no doubt that the flight of the *Plus Ultra* was a national and a worldwide accomplishment and for many a surprise. What a contrast this adventurous spirit was

Franco and his crew with the King of Spain, Alfonso XIII. (A.B.C.)

with the low morale of the year 1898! We were rising again, holding the red and yellow standard which the Spanish Army had never let fall and were presenting it as a symbol of our race and the unknown crusade of sacrifice which Spanish Aviation was making towards historic progress. This flight proved to all that Spain was still standing. From that moment the Spanish knew that aviation was admirable and Franco was an idol'.

Much was made of the similarity of the venture with the voyage of Columbus, especially when Major Franco announced that the flight would start from Palos de Moguer near Huelva whence Columbus had departed on his first voyage on 3 August 1492. The aircraft was named *Plus Ultra* — 'Farther Still' — the title which Charles V had adopted for the discovery of America, so contradicting the legendary 'Ne Plus Ultra — Thus far and no farther' — the ancient view of the Pillars of Hercules.

On the eve of the flight, 21 January, the famous pedagogue Don Manuel Siarot gave forth:

'Over the schools of Huelva full of majesty flew the hydroplane of oceanic dreams. Inside its iron body go the luminous thoughts of science, the charm of youth and Spanish sacrifice

On leaving Palos, it is not an airplane that takes off, it is the caravel *Santa Maria* which has miraculously changed its sails for wings. Columbus and his sailors have become

Enthusiasm in Buenos Aires.
(A.B.C.)

The flying-boat 'Plus Ultra'
afloat. (A.B.C.)

airmen. The spirit of our race on this morning of glory is called Franco.

Don Quixote has learned science and can now make an ideal a reality by constructing life with science and romance, the supreme formula for progress. Don Quixote sends out the caravel and in Palos, in La Rábida, on the sea and in America tears fall from the eyes on contemplating Spain's labours towards the world's civilising destinies.

When Franco's plane left Africa it was the incarnation of an army restored by its own sacrifices for civilisation; since touching down on the waters of the Tinto and the Odiel it has merged with the sacred oils of all the greatness of our race.

Make way for the *Santa Maria* of the air. More than a hundred million Spanish speakers urge it on.

Brothers of Columbus[1] now on board this sacred craft tell our American brothers it is part of Spain eternal and that Palos, La Rábida and Huelva are watching this treasure of the first page of the world.

Make way for the caravel of the sky. It is being guided by God'.

Amid all this oratory and enthusiasm the flying boat was being carefully tested at the Air Force Mar Chica base at Melilla in Spanish North Africa, and by mid-January 1926 when the air crew went to say goodbye to the King and the Government in Madrid all was ready and Franco was confident. After a flurry of parties they flew to the River Odiel near Huelva on the mainland of Spain on 19 January. Next day they rested and, like Columbus before them, went to pray at the Monastery of La Rábida.

At dawn on 22 January after hearing Mass at La Rábida before the altar of the Virgen Milagrosa they went out to the *Plus Ultra* and got aboard — Major Franco, Captain Ruiz de Alda, Naval Lieut. Durán, mechanic Rada and the photographer Alonso as a

[1]Perhaps it is not unfair to recall that Columbus was an Italian from Genoa.

Franco's Dornier 'Whale'.
(Musée de l'Air)

passenger. The heir to the throne and countless personages came to see them off. At 7.47 am the Napier engines were started and three minutes later they were away. They carried with them letters from the King to the Presidents of Brazil, Uruguay and Argentina, a gold cup from the Columbian Society to be presented to the 'The first magistrate of the Argentine Republic', and an emotional address from the Press Associations of Huelva, Madrid and all Spain to their American brothers[1].

After circling the Columbus monument at La Rábida they put out to sea accompanied by an escort of another Dornier as far as the African coast.

Following the path of Sacadura Cabral and Gago Coutinho the first stage was as far as Las Palmas in the Canaries. This stage of the journey was uneventful although there was a lot of cloud but their wireless contacts worked very well and put them in position right over Las Palmas. A small repair was needed here and it was not until 26 January that they took off for the Cape Verde Islands. To lighten the aircraft the reporter Alonso was put off at Las Palmas and a lesser load of petrol was carried. They had feared poor visibility on the second leg of the flight but the direction-finding radio worked admirably and by picking up signals from Porto Praia and São Vicente were able to come down at Porto Praia as planned, though in poor visibility and a rough sea. The first stage of 1315 km had taken 8 hours and the second of 1745 km took 9 hrs 50 mins and set a new record for waterplanes in distance and speed.

In the Cape Verde Islands they unloaded all unnecessary spares and equipment and some necessary ones including some smoke cans for drift observation, provisions, boxes of gifts and tools; they also off-loaded Lt. Durán on to the destroyer *Alsedo* so as to carry as much fuel as possible for the stage across the Atlantic. They also changed propellers. The original plan had been to carry enough fuel to make the full journey to Recife but the difficulties they feared in taking off from a rough sea made them reduce the stage to that 'airman's friend', the island of Fernando Noronha. The *Alsedo* went

[1]Among the stores carried on board was a box of provisions including 5 kg of dried figs, 2 kg of ham, 2 kg of sugar, 1 kg of cocoa and 1 kg of coffee, 3 kg of biscuits, 1 bottle of brandy and one of sherry, a vacuum flask and a water distiller.

on ahead and the cruiser *Blas de Lezo* with other spares and gear on board remained with the plane to give help and back-up.

Having missed the January moon they resolved to leave at first light and take off from the Barrera do Inferno near Porto Praia where they hoped for some protection from the weather. The *Blas de Lezo's* launch towed them out, with the tow ropes parting several times, but finally at 6.11 am on 30 January after some difficulties they got away.

The journey does not seem to have been too hideous; they flew between clouds at 300 metres over a very rough sea. For four hours they were out of touch with world but at 2 pm they could hear shipping. Once they went through a tropical shower which drenched them. They picked up the Pernambuco (Recife) radio and then at sunset there was their island ahead. They alighted at 6.35 pm alongside a British ship and taxied some 20 miles towards the island lighthouse which was lit by then. It was too rough to go alongside the dock and after one failure they anchored and decided to spend an uncomfortable night aboard the aircraft. The stage had occupied 12 hrs 40 mins and covered 2305 km. Next day the *Alsedo* arrived and the *Plus Ultra* recovered her missing stores and parcels and re-embarked Lt. Durán.

In the words of Ruiz de Alda: 'On this short stage' — the 540 km to Recife — 'we suffered a grave accident. The propeller of the rear engine broke. We had to stop it but the front engine was not powerful enough (to hold height) and we had to come down to sea level. We had to throw everything overboard including our luggage. Franco managed to stay airborne but at times they touched the waves; it was only as their fuel load lessened that they could gain any height. Ruiz de Alda continues: 'Our arrival in Pernambuco (Recife) made up for the bad experience. We flew at a height lower than the coconut trees of the coast. For over 100 km the shore was occupied by natives, mostly blacks, awaiting the arrival of *Plus Ultra*. After this chase along the coast we arrived at Pernambuco where an indescribable welcome awaited us. Thousands of Spaniards who live there and who hardly remember our language hugged us, filled with emotion'. This stage on 31 January was 540 km occupying 3 hrs 38 min.

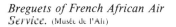

Breguets of French African Air Service. (Musée de l'Air)

So was the South Atlantic first crossed by a single aeroplane between 22 and 31 January 1926.

Two further records lay ahead, a non-stop flight from Recife to Rio de Janeiro, 2100 km, and another non-stop from Rio to Montevideo. The first of these was achieved on 4 February in 12 hrs 16 mins. Ruiz de Alda commented: 'The trip to Rio de Janeiro was "tourism" and the only thing worth mentioning is the strength of the pilot who flew for 12 hours . . . At Rio we saw the most formidable spectacle imaginable, the unparalleled Bay was full of every kind of boat and shone brightly with a myriad of colours. The landing was very difficult because of all the obstacles which endangered our plane. One of the many boats that wanted to sail beside us managed to break our rudder. There was such a crowd to welcome us that it took us three hours to cover the 1 km distance to the hotel. We expected a welcome in the Argentine but were surprised by the Brazilian welcome'.

After the most fulsome displays of love, admiration and excitement during which Franco lost a lock of hair and Rada had his arm dislocated, the *Plus Ultra* was able to leave.

The use of a two-bladed propeller and unsuitable petrol combined to make the two take-off attempts from Rio both long and dangerous. Once airborne they realised that Buenos Aires was out of range and were contemplating coming down in Rio Grande do Sul but picked up a favourable wind and made it into Montevideo. This arrival was as tumultuous as the others with huge crowds and unprecedented enthusiasm.

They took off next day for the short flight to Buenos Aires but almost immediately descended with a petrol leak; they switched tanks and took off again. In just over the hour they were in Buenos Aires and the great flight was over. As before, enormous crowds and unimaginable enthusiasm greeted them.

The stages covered by the *Plus Ultra* were as follows:

Date	Stage	Kms	Flying time
22.1.26	Palos to Las Palmas	1300	8 hrs
26.1.26.	Las Palmas to Porto Praia	1745	9 hrs 50 mins
30.1.26	Porto Praia to Fernando Noronha	2305	12 hrs 40 mins
31.1.26	Fernando Noronha to Recife	540	3 hrs 38 mins
4.2.26	Recife to Rio de Janeiro	2100	12 hrs 16 mins
9.2.26	Rio de Janeiro to Montevideo	2060	12 hr 5 mins
10.2.26	Montevideo to Buenos Aires	220	1 hr 11 mins
		10270	50 hrs 50 mins

Franco telegraphed to the King saying: 'The reception has been enthusiastic; I think we shall leave the City alive. Everything was done for Your Majesty and Spain'. Alfonso XIII replied: 'I am delighted that the *Plus Ultra* "raid" has been successful. I have pleasure in congratulating you and granting you, Ruiz de Alda, and

Rescue of Major Franco by H.M.S. 'Eagle' in 1929; he had been at sea for seven days.
(Illustrated London News)

Durán the order of "Llave de Gentilhombre[1]" reserving how to show my gratitude to Rada'.

The Chilean writer Emilio Rodriguez Mendoza, on behalf of the Latin American Diplomatic Corps in Madrid, sent this message:

> 'Serenity has not died in Spain in face of danger, heroic faith before strong endeavour, audacity before death. Indeed they combine with Major Franco and his companions the magnificent epoch with which Spain traced one of the greatest steps of any of the nations. If yesterday Spain was the first to arrive with unfurled sails in the New World, today she is the first to arrive with open wings in search of her children. The *Plus Ultra* symbolises the genius of our race and, winging over the abyss and distance as a triumphal annunciation has just brought again to America the most eternal verities of the Spanish soul. Your immortal flight perfects the spiritual union of our race, covering with winged shadow into the future the imprint of Columbus and the explorers'.

In rather drier style Sir Samuel Hoare, the British Air Minister, telegraphed the Spanish Ministry of War saying: 'The Air Council have learned with great pleasure of the successful completion of the transatlantic flight by Commandante Franco and Captain Alda. They desire to offer the Spanish Army Air Service cordial congratulations on a most brilliant achievement'.

[1]Virtually untranslatable; 'The Key of Gentlemanliness' perhaps, or 'The Key of Chivalry'.

Major Franco's flying-boat on the water after rescue by H.M.S. 'Eagle', 1929.
(Illustrated London News)

As soon as the immediate excitement had subsided Franco and his team were planning the return journey which was intended to be via Chile, Mexico, Cuba and the Azores, but the Spanish Government decided that the 'raid' should end in Buenos Aires and presented the *Plus Ultra* to the Argentine nation as a mark of Hispanic brotherhood. The heroes returned home as guests of the Argentine Navy in the cruiser *Buenos Aires*.

The ultimate fate of the crew of the *Plus Ultra* was a sad one, only Rada living to any age. He died in the sanatorium of Las Molinas in Madrid in April 1969 near the age of 67. He had the luck to survive after the Civil War in spite of having been a leader of anarchist hooligans who specialised in burning down churches. He also flew the Atlantic during the Civil War with a consignment of money. Durán was killed in a flying accident while on manoeuvres with the Navy near Valencia on 17 July 1926, having had barely three months to enjoy his success. Ruiz de Alda became involved in extreme right wing politics, was locked up at the outbreak of the Civil War and later murdered by the Reds in the massacre of political prisoners at the Model Prison in Madrid on 23/24 August 1936.[1]

Franco was a strange character, rebellious, proud, aloof, ambitious, moody, and pig-headed — nicknamed 'The Jackal' by his friends; he was a fine pilot and very much a loner. His two disastrous marriages were no help. On 1 August 1928 he set off in a four-engined Dornier 'Super Whale' to fly around the world; this flight failed at once with damage to the hull. A second attempt was approved by the Spanish Government provided he used a Spanish-built Dornier Wal from the Cadiz factory. Franco regarded the local machine with distaste and preferred a German-built machine which was at hand. He therefore switched the identifying numbers

[1] See the *The Spanish Civil War* by Hugh Thomas — Pelican Books.

and on 21 July 1929 he took off in the falsified plane for the Azores with Gallarza, Ruiz de Alda and mechanic Madariaga. On the next day he missed the Azores and came down on the sea. He was lost and amid great national grief a huge search was mounted by several nations. With a bad storm on 24 July hopes of finding him were fading but on the 29th he and his plane were reported safe and sound on the British aircraft carrier HMS *Eagle*.

For this Franco got into severe trouble and he was cashiered and imprisoned. There were ugly rumours that Dornier had offered money if the German machine was used. Later Franco became disillusioned with the monarchy and 'bombarded' the palace area of Madrid with leaflets supporting a Republic. By 1936 he was against the Republic and on the side of his brothers in the Civil War.

Ramón Franco was killed during the war on 28 October 1938. According to his friend Bartolomé Sagrera he took off from Majorca in a three-engined Cant seaplane on a day of violent storm to bomb the docks at Valencia. It was so rough on that day that one aircraft sank at its moorings. Franco's plane was seen to be in trouble and it turned away to the North as if to return to base, disappeared into heavy cloud and was lost. His body was recovered next day.

11.
Italian Nobleman

After Franco's highly successful flight in the early months of 1926, activity died down over North and South Atlantic alike until September when René Fonck made his disastrous attempt from New York. Next in the field was a Brazilian team, with an Italian Savoia-Marchetti S55 flying boat, modified for the flight, named *Jaú*. They left Genoa on 17 October 1926. The Captain was Commandant João de Barros who had with him Capt. Newton Braga as navigator, Sr. Artur Cunha as co-pilot and a mechanic Vasco Cinquini.

The Savoia-Marchetti S55 was a sturdy, ugly and highly successful flying boat — as was the German Dornier Wal — and it had a long life in production. The first one flew in 1924. Not only did the Marquis of Pinedo make a highly successful passage of the Atlantic in one, as is described in this chapter, but Marshal Italo Balbo led a mass flight of 24 of them from Italy to the World Fair in Chicago and back in 1933, after an earlier and smaller mass flight to Rio de Janeiro in January 1931. The S55 was a twin-hulled flying boat with a single thick cantilever wing with a span of 24 metres (78 ft 8 ins) with a considerable taper. Above the wing, supported by a stout group of struts were two engines in tandem — as in the Dornier Wal — with a single radiator in front. The tail unit, supported by booms leading out from the stern of the boat bodies, consisted of a single elevator and triple rudders. A choice of engines was possible and for their flight the Brazilians chose two 500 hp Isotta-Fraschini motors.

The pilots sat in the wing, side by side, immediately below the engines. The mechanics' quarters were in the hulls which were joined by a tunnel containing instruments and auxiliary gear such as pumps. The hulls also carried the fuel and naval accessories, like anchors. On each side of each hull were portholes. The aircraft were built in timber and plywood with some fabric coverings.

The *Jaú*, after leaving Genoa, was forced down with engine trouble at Alicante. Here the authorities, who had no prior knowledge of de Barros and his flight, locked the aviators up in the city jail whence they were released by the intervention of the Brazilian Ambassador. They reached Gibraltar on 19 October

Savoia-Marchetti S55 flying-boat.
(Royal Aeronautical Society)

where the engines were overhauled and moved on to Las Palmas on 25 October where further engine repairs were needed. They were then forced down at the Island of Fogo in the Cape Verde Islands, near Porto Praia. So it was 8 November before they reached Porto Praia, to take stock of their position. Here the flight was nearly abandoned because of a conflict between de Barros and Cunha over command. Cunha returned home and a new co-pilot was shipped by sea from Brazil, Lt. João Negrão, a member of the São Paulo police force, who had never piloted a flying boat. De Barros returned to Italy to obtain spare parts.

Finally the plane left Porto Praia on 28 April 1927 but had to make a forced descent into the sea off Fernando Noronha; they were rescued by an Italian ship and towed into the 'Aviators Haven' for more repairs. Here Commandant de Barros, still undaunted by many troubles caused by foreign matter in the fuel, put the *Jaú* back into working order and resumed his flight to the Brazilian mainland. This he achieved on 14 May, coming down first at Port Natal and then at Recife (Pernambuco). According to the *New York Times:*

> 'Despite these delays and repeated erroneous reports that they had landed, the enthusiasm today was unbounded when the flyers arrived . . . A report that incompetence was responsible for the fall of the plane into the sea caused a serious riot in Rio de Janeiro on April 25th where one person was killed'.

The *Jaú* arrived just before Lindbergh took off in the *Spirit of St. Louis* so de Barros and his crew just qualify as pre-Lindbergh pioneers.

In the 1920s and 1930s the Italians were very much a force to be reckoned with in aviation, making long-distance flights in their own Savoia S55s or locally-built Dorniers and competing for the Schneider Trophy with fast seaplanes. In these activities the armed forces took a full part.

The Marquese de Pinedo.
(Associated Newspapers)

Among the most conspicuous military pilots was Colonel the Marquis of Pinedo, a member of a noble Neapolitan family. He had done well in the war and subsequently made his reputation as a world flyer by his trip from Italy to Australia, followed by his circumnavigation of the continent. After substantial repairs in Sydney he flew to Japan and from there across China and India back to Italy. Pinedo used a single-engined Savoia S16 biplane flying boat *Il Genneriello,* and was accompanied by Ernesto Campanelli as mechanic and co-pilot. For this exploit he was awarded the first Gold Medal of the Fédération Aéronautique Internationale.

Pinedo's next plan was the ambitious one of a double crossing of the Atlantic; first from east to west from Africa to South America, then — after visiting the intervening countries and showing the flag to the large colonies of Italian-born Americans — from Newfoundland to Europe via the Azores. This in fact he accomplished with some vicissitudes. His crossing of the South Atlantic falls within our arbitrary limit of the date of Lindbergh's flight, and his crossing of the North Atlantic just outside it.

Pinedo chose a Savoia-Marchetti S55 flying boat with twin Isotta-Fraschini Asso 500 hp engines. For crew he chose Captain Carlo del Prete as second pilot and navigator with Vitale Zacchetti as mechanic. The aircraft was named *Santa Maria* after Columbus's flagship.

The plane was by no means easy to fly, difficult when taking off with a full load, particularly so in flat calm and high air temperatures. In these conditions the boat could not always climb on to the 'steps' of the hulls and persistent driving then on full throttle could overheat the engines. This meant another try when things were cooler or removing fuel, which meant greater risks or shorter flight stages. Taking off into a swell with a crosswind was also disagreeable. The necessity to keep at almost full throttle for some time after a full load take-off was also an anxiety. Spray and tropical rain also created problems by pitting and eroding the propellers, which reduced power.

The pilots' open cabin turned out to be surprisingly unpleasant; a helmet and goggles were necessary at all times and were uncomfortable in the tropics; rain came in and sea water drenched them at take-off and landing. There was also the risk of objects flying out and hitting the rear propeller.

With these shortcomings the *Santa Maria* was a stout, sturdy ship and but for a wildly unlucky accident would probably have completed the round trip.

The Marquis left the Savoia Works at Sesto Calende on Lake Maggiore on 8 February 1927 and flew to the seaplane base at Cagliari in Sardinia where the journey officially started on 13 February with a flight of 1000 miles to Kenitra (Rabat) in Morocco. Next day Pinedo flew 1000 miles, first to Villa Cisneros in Spanish

The disastrous fire which destroyed Pinedo's flying-boat at the Roosevelt dam.
(Illustrated London News)

Sahara, and later that evening carried on by moonlight reaching Bolama in Portuguese Guinea next morning, 15 February.

Pinedo had intended to fly the South Atlantic in one stage from Bolama to Natal but the difficulties of take-off were too great — seven attempts to take off with enough fuel to reach the Brazilian coast had failed — so the Italians flew back to Dakar on 18 February and then to Porto Praia in the Cape Verde Islands on 19 February to shorten the transatlantic stage.

At Porto Praia the difficulties of take-off continued and several attempts failed. At last after reducing their fuel and food to a minimum they got away about 1 am on 22 February. They had a grim flight of 15 hrs and 15 mins as on reaching the coast of Brazil they could not put down because of storm conditions and rough seas and had to go back to Fernando Noronha, once more the Aviator's Friend. This was the toughest day for the crew: not only were they facing fatigue but also nervous tension after their efforts to take off from Bolama and Porto Praia. In addition they encountered frequent squalls on this stage. However on 24 February they got across to Port Natal and Recife

After the big jump the *Santa Maria* continued to Bahia and Rio de Janeiro, which was reached on 27 February, then southwards to Santos and on 1 March to Porto Alegre. Buenos Aires was reached on 2 March.

At Buenos Aires they had a thorough overhaul and changed

engines but on 14 March they were off again, flying to Asuncion in Paraguay via Montevideo and Paraná. Then they had a hazardous and stormy stage over the 'green hell' of central Brazil, hitherto unflown, to San Luis de Caceres, Guaiara Mirim, Manaos on the Amazon and Belém (Pará) at its mouth. Thence up the Guyanas via Paramaribo and Georgetown, to Pointe à Pitre in Guadaloupe and Port au Prince in Haiti to Havana. New Orleans was reached on 29 March. Here Pinedo changed his plans in order to visit the west coast of the United States at San Diego, Los Angeles, San Francisco and Seattle and then fly across the continent.

On 2 April the *Santa Maria* set off for the west and with stops at Galveston, Lake Medina and Hot Springs, reached the Roosevelt Dam lake in Arizona on 5 April.

Here came tragedy. While the *Santa Maria* was preparing to leave Roosevelt Dam after being refuelled two local boys approached in a rowing boat and lighting a cigarette threw the burning match over the side; this ignited some spilled petrol on the surface of the water

Savoia flying-boat in air.
(Musée de l'Air)

and within seconds the aircraft was a blazing wreck destroyed by a fire 'appiccato la un inprudente giovane indigeno[1]'.

The United States Government immediately offered an aircraft for Pinedo to complete this flight but he preferred to wait for a replacement from Italy, an identical S55 which reached New York by boat in the fast time of $3\frac{1}{2}$ weeks. This enabled him to take-off for Boston on 2 May in *Santa Maria II* bearing the motto 'Post fata resurgo'. While waiting for the new machine the US Navy had flown the Italians to San Diego (where Del Prete survived a forced landing), Los Angeles and San Francisco to receive the love and admiration of the Italian communities everywhere; they also fitted in trips to Washington and New York. From Boston, starting on 9 May they flew back to New Orleans to resume their flight path with stops at Norwalk, New York, Philadelphia, Charleston and

[1]"Caused by a careless young local boy" from *Cieli e Mari* by Capani (U. Mursia) 1973.

Pensacola in Florida. From New Orleans they flew up the Mississippi with a call at Memphis to Chicago, then to Montreal, Quebec, to Rimouski down the St. Lawrence, and on to Shippigan with some fog problems. The *Santa Maria II* reached Trepassey Bay, Newfoundland, its take-off point for the transatlantic flight on 20 May, the day that Lindbergh left for Paris.

Checking over his aircraft for the Atlantic flight Pinedo was held up until 23 May and so lost the favourable winds that had helped Lindbergh. Instead with crosswinds which made him cut down his fuel load Pinedo left at 3.45 am hoping to reach Flores, the nearest island in the Azores. But he ran into head winds and realising that these and rising seas would prevent their reaching even Flores, Pinedo put the *Santa Maria II* down that afternoon close to a Portuguese ship *L'Infanta da Sagres* still 280 km short of the nearest island, and accepted a tow. According to one account indeed his first tug was a schooner. The flying boat was very hard to handle in tow and on 26 May they exchanged their first tug for the Italian steamer *Superga* which on 30 May reached the port of Horta in the Azores. The *Santa Maria II* was little damaged and by 10 June was able to take off from Horta to fly back to where they had come down on the sea so as to miss out no part of the Atlantic flight — as Cabral and Coutinho had done in 1922 — and then came down to Ponta Delgada. Next day they left the Azores and flying via Lisbon and Barcelona (whence Pinedo went to Madrid at the request of the King of Spain) reached the Lido of Ostia close by Rome on 16 June.

The whole of Italy was in ecstasy over Pinedo's return and Rome and other cities were decorated in his honour. He himself was promoted to the rank of General, at the age of 37. *Flight* said 'that he had thus concluded what must certainly be recorded as — next perhaps to the Round-the-World flight — the greatest flight made in the history of aviation'. The British Ambassador wrote to Signor Mussolini as follows:

> 'By direction of His Majesty King George V I am honoured in asking Your Excellency to pray His Majesty the King of Italy to permit the bestowing on Colonel the Marchese de Pinedo of the Air Force Cross. It is with the deepest pleasure that I convey the proposal of giving the greatest flier the highest decoration that can be conferred on a British aviator. British men followed Colonel de Pinedo's latest feat with the utmost interest, and also recall his previous flight when he landed at several British ports where he left an unforgettable record behind him of sportsmanship, frankness, unpretentiousness, skilfulness and efficiency'.

Although Pinedo continued to enjoy the warmest affection of the Italian public — it is reported for example that he was uproariously acclaimed when he arrived in Venice to see Britain and Italy contest

The Savoia-Marchetti S55.
(Musée de l'Air)

the Schneider Trophy in 1927 — he fell foul of the upper crust of Italian society and was the object of 'intense jealousy' in certain official circles; one explanation was that he became attracted by King Victor Emmanuel's daughter Princess Giovanna and that the affection was returned; there was also a row about money[1]. Probably there was not room in Italy's Hall of Heroes for both Pinedo and Marshal Italo Balbo so that the senior man got rid of the junior. At any rate the Marquis was shipped off to the Argentine as Ambassador where he languished until 1933. In August of that year he was approached by Hugo D'Annunzio, the son of the famous wild soldier and poet, and asked to attempt the world's long-distance record which stood at $5653\frac{1}{2}$ miles set by Rossi and Codos.

Pinedo agreed and reached Floyd Bennett Field in New York to take over a new Bellanca monoplane. On 2 September 1933 with the intention of flying to Baghdad he tried to take off with the monstrous load about of about four tons of petrol. Swerving all over the runway the Bellanca failed to rise, swung away and crashed into a fence. Pinedo struggled out of his seat and had almost reached safety when he was engulfed in flames and so perished.

[1] See F. H. and E. Ellis in *Atlantic Air Conquest* — Wm. Kimber 1963.

12.
Portuguese by Night and French Enigma

Three flights remain to be described before Lindbergh took off and so put all the other attempts in the shade. One of these, the attempt to fly the South Atlantic non-stop by the French crew of de Saint Roman in their Farman Goliath in May 1927, had strangely enough an ambiguous ending — the only uncertain ending to any of the attempts on either North or South Atlantic crossings up to that time.

Before that, in February 1927, there had been a Uruguayan attempt which ended in bad trouble off the African coast and then in March came a successful Portuguese flight across the South Atlantic.

The Uruguayan team was led by Commandant Larre Borges with Capt. Ibarra as second pilot and navigator, his brother Capt. Larre Borges as wireless operator and a mechanic named Rigoli. The intention was to fly to Montevideo and then around the world. They flew a Dornier Wal flying boat, with two 500 hp Farman engines.

The Dornier 'Whale' flying-boat.
(Real Photo/Ian Allan)

They left Pisa on 20 February intending to fly via Dakar and Pernambuco; they called at Alicante and Casablanca but on their way south to Dakar they were forced down by a broken oil pipe off the coast of Spanish Sahara. They came down in the trough of the waves, were hit broadside on and their plane was flung on to the beach and wrecked. The crew then had a half-hour fight with the surf to get ashore. A razzia, or band of armed marauders, arrived on the scene — much of the Sahara was unsubdued then — sacked the plane, stripped the crew and forced them on foot to their village of Puerto Cansado across the hot sands of the desert, the chief brigand splendid in captured silk pyjamas. Here no doubt the Moors were of two minds between ransom and murder. But help was on the way from the pilots of the famous French Latécoère Air Line, which had the arduous and risky job of flying the mails between Casablanca and Dakar and in later years across to South America. Some famous pilots flew this route including the great Mermoz and Antoine de Saint Exupéry. Two French planes found the wreck of the Dornier and news from the fort at Cape Juby located the whereabouts of the prisoners. The first expedition, a week after the wreck, was greeted by rifle fire but the French planes were back next day, made a quick pick-up and roared away.

The next attempt in 1927 on the South Atlantic was successful; this was the east to west flight of the Portuguese team of Sarmento Beires in March. The remainder of the crew consisted of Jorge de Castilho, navigator, Lt. Manuel Gouveia, mechanic, and Major Dovalle Portugal, second pilot. The aircraft was yet again a Dornier Wal with two 450 hp Lorraine-Dietrich engines; it was named *Argos*.

They left Lisbon on 3 March and stopping at Casablanca and Villa Cisneros they reached Bolama in Portuguese Guinea on 6 March. Here they had serious difficulties in getting off the water with a full load. They finally got away on 11 March having left Lt. Gouveia behind. They stopped again at Soga on Brissagos Island in Portuguese Guinea. Here they shed their second pilot, Major Dovalle Portugal, and Beires and de Castilho made the Atlantic crossing unaccompanied. Yet again Portuguese navigation was first class for they made the long, long crossing to Fernando Noronha (once more) in 18 hours 12 minutes and overnight at that — the first night flight across the Atlantic — on 16-17 March. Next day they reached Port Natal and then via Recife and Bahia where a propeller was damaged. Later the flight to Rio de Janeiro was completed. A salute of ten guns was fired in Lisbon.

Sarmento Beires had originally intended to attempt an around-the-world flight but the Portuguese Government vetoed this on account of expense and also a return flight across the Atlantic. The *Argos* was ordered to make for North America. They left Rio, made their way up the coast and were wrecked at Georgetown in British Guiana where they had a forced landing in which their flying boat sank.

Crew of the 'Argos', a Dornier 'Whale' led by Sarmento Beires; the first team to fly the South Atlantic by night.
(Naval Museum, Lisbon)

Although the South Atlantic had been crossed by air four times by the spring of 1927 there were still new records to break or around-the-world flights to be brought off. One of the chief goals not yet attained was a direct non-stop flight from continent to continent, either from Europe or from Africa to South America.

The French, who had been developing air traffic to their African empire since World War I, had rather surprisingly not been involved in an attempt on the South Atlantic until quite late in the day, although they did pull off the first mainland to mainland flight. The intriguing question is, which French team brought it off? The credit has always gone in the literature to Costes and Le Brix who crossed non-stop from Dakar in Senegal to Natal in northern Brazil on 14-15 October 1927 in a military long-range Breguet XIX named *Nungesser et Coli* in honour of France's heroes lost in the North Atlantic in May of that year.

Recently, however, the suggestion has been raised[1] by P. Lissarrague that the first non-stop flight across the South Atlantic was in fact achieved earlier in that same year by the team of Captain Pierre de Serre de Saint Roman with Lieutenant Mouneyres and mechanic-quartermaster Petit.

So far it had always been assumed that they were lost at sea and if indeed they did get across, as P. Lissarrague's article maintains, they certainly did not live to tell the tale and no trace of them was ever found. It is on the evidence of some wreckage picked up off the coast of Brazil 43 days after they had left Africa that the case for the success rests.

de Saint Roman was a brave and distinguished soldier in the

[1] In the October 1977 issue of *Pegase,* the journal of the Friends of the French Musée de L'Air.

Dornier 'Wal' or 'Whale' flying-boat in the air. (Musée de l'Air)

French Army in World War I. In 1918 he transferred to the Flying Corps and was a qualified pilot by August, but the war ended before he had been in action. After the war he left the Service and joined a commercial firm where he conceived the idea of taking an aircraft across the South Atlantic by sea to be followed by a goodwill and trade-promotion aerial tour of 52 South American cities. From this it was only a step to add to the plan the crossing of the South Atlantic by plane as well. The Paris-Latin American Society were attracted by the idea and put up some money — de Saint Roman had none — and the Farman Company agreed to provide one of their Goliath twin-engined biplanes with Lorraine-Dietrich supporting the project with the necessary engines. De Saint Roman was possibly short of experience with only 253 hours of flying on his record but his fellow pilot Mouneyres, who was planning a flight to New York for the spring of 1927, had had 1200 hours on airships and aeroplanes. With them they planned to take the Lorraine-Dietrich mechanic Mathis and an Argentine journalist Carlos del Carril.

The Farman Goliath was a well-tried aircraft, developed as a bomber in World War I. With a span of 91 ft it was rather larger than a Vickers Vimy, though decidedly slower. It was used by both the French Army and Navy for some years after the war as a bomber and the civil version was widely used as an airliner with 14 seats.

The Goliath was ready early in April and was named *Paris-Amérique Latine;* it was flown from Le Bourget to St. Raphael in the South of France and fitted with floats. On 10 April the test pilot Drouhin then flew it to Berre near Marseille and made some full-load take-offs. After the hand-over de Saint Roman tried it satisfactorily and flew it to Casablanca without incident on 16 April. It was ready to leave for St. Louis in Senegal next day but at the first attempt Mouneyres could not get off the water, so after discharging 200 litres of petrol de Saint Roman tried again. This time, just as he was taking off, a wave damaged the base of one of the floats and one of the propellers, so de Saint Roman beached the aircraft.

This experience decided him to abandon floats and fly his Farman as a land-plane, putting back the original wheels. This change-over took a few days and in this period the Men from the Ministry sent a characteristically ambiguous message warning de Saint Roman that if his plane was not fitted with floats it did not comply with 'navigability conditions', although the normal condition for the Goliath was with wheels. The Ministry also tried in vain to press the Paris-Latin American Association to stop de Saint Roman; then the Argentine Ambassador ordered del Carril off the plane and Mathis the mechanic withdrew, uncertain of his insurance. However, Mouneyres met a mechanic he knew in Casablanca called Petit who at once agreed to join the expedition.

de Saint Roman was ready to go and on 2 May 1927 had an excellent flight to St. Louis in Senegal with a stop at Agadir. This flight showed improved speed and fuel economy over the performance earlier when fitted with floats. Another discouraging telegram greeted the party here but the aviators decided that as theirs was a private flight they could not be stopped and would carry on.

With good weather reported from Recife on 4 May, *Paris-Amerique Latine* took off easily at 7.15 am on 5 May. Up to 11.35 am they were heard on radio at St. Louis and Dakar. After that, silence.

There were unconfirmed reports of the flight at St. Paul's Rocks and Fernando Noronha but as Lissarrague says, 'toujours les fausses nouvelles qui accompagnent les drames'.

On 7 May the Brazilian Government sent a ship, the *Mercury,* along the coast from Recife as far north as Cabo Roque and a few days later a destroyer was sent eastward to St. Paul's Rocks — nothing was found. France mourned another loss to add to the agony of Nungesser and Coli and the flight was castigated as unauthorised and foolhardy.

Then on 18 June, forty-three days after the disappearance of de Saint Roman, some Brazilian fishermen found a strange raft 50

Farman 'Goliath' of de Saint Roman.
(Musée de l'Air)

miles off Cabo Marguarinho near the estuary of the Para River and the City of Belem. In a statement to the French Consul in Belem, the fishermen said that the raft was a large rectangle of fabric stretched over a frame — which could readily be diagnosed as an aileron — to which were attached two spoked wheels and an inspection hatch ('porte de visite ronde') in duralumin by means of elastic cords ('sandows'). Attempts were made to tow the raft but with the sea rising the sailors had to abandon towing, cut the cords and bring the pieces with them. The Consul was able to consult a former Goliath mechanic who reached Belem on 14 July. He was quite positive that the wreckage was from a Goliath judging from the marks and numbers on the tyres. Nothing however indicated what the raft was really intended to be as it was too small to have supported three men.

The French Foreign Office then had the debris brought back to France for examination by the Farman Company; it arrived on 7 December. The experts there were sure that the wheels came from de St. Roman's plane and that the hubs, rims and spokes showed no signs of violent shock; the covers and inner tubes were not scraped or cut and they believed that the wheels had been removed from their axle with a tool and not torn off. Mr Prado of Farman's concluded that the aircraft had landed normally and that the wheels had been removed after landing.

From here on the mystery takes over from the facts. The raft was found nearly 1300 nautical miles from Recife, for which the Goliath was bound, nor had the plane the range to have reached the spot where the raft was found. However there are currents along the Brazilian coast setting north-west parallel to the shore north of Cabo St. Roque and south-west south of the Cape; these currents run at one to three knots.

The inference is that the plane was off course and that after coming down on the shore north of Cabo St. Roque broke up or was broken up deliberately and that the parts which were found had drifted north along the coastline. It could also be inferred that if the first search had gone beyond Cabo St. Roque the *Paris-Amerique Latine* might have been discovered. It seems strange none the less that no other traces could be found. It is true that it is an inhospitable coast with few remote fishing villages and a deserted interior, large stretches of which are cut off by steep cliffs from the shore. The tides run from three to ten feet with occasionally sudden tidal waves at a greater height.

The Goliath should have reached Recife at 00.30 local time on 6 May and low tide was at 2 am and high tide at 9 am that morning. With the plane off course to the north and running short of fuel Lissarrague believes that they made a forced landing on the beach north of Cabo St. Roque and that the plane was wrecked by the rising tide where cliffs shut off the land. So the aviators who had made the non-stop crossing made up a raft to carry a message — to

Farman 'Goliath' fitted with floats. (Musée de l'Air)

make a 'bouteille de mer' as it were — and direct rescuers to their position.

There is a case for this hypothesis and the suggestion of a bottle with a message consigned to the deep is attractive. Alternatives suggest themselves: the plane might have come down in the sea, the survivors, one, two or three, might have got ashore, the plane washed up on a later tide perhaps. A sole survivor might have made a raft and been drowned. The verdict would seem to be Not Proven.

13.
The World's Hero

After starting research for this chapter on the fiftieth anniversary of the very day on which Lindbergh took off for Paris from Roosevelt Field, New York, it was a wonderful coincidence to hear a neighbour Mary Kent say 'I was there'. She went on: 'The ground was soft and the plane seemed overloaded; we thought he'd never get off. At the last as we were all digging our nails into the palms of our hands he struggled into the air, just cleared the wires at the end of the field and was on his way'. And she added, 'My sister Lucy was in Paris and saw him arrive'. The *New York Times* wrote in the same vein: 'And then slowly, so slowly that those watching it stood fascinated, as if by indomitable will alone the young pilot lifted the plane.'

So began what became the most famous flight in history, first in so many things though not the first to cross the Atlantic, but the longest then from point to point by far and of course the first *solo*.

'Wasn't it wonderful that he did it alone!' said Mrs Charles F. Kettering. 'It would have been much more wonderful if he'd done it with a committee', replied her husband. In a way both these remarks are true; it was indeed wonderful that he did it alone if only in that he had to stay awake for $33\frac{1}{2}$ hours, but the fact that he had conceived and organised the entire enterprise himself without the interference and compromises of a shared project, that all the decisions and risks of the flight were his alone must have clarified and simplified the task immensely. As he himself wrote years afterwards:[1]

> 'By flying alone I've gained in range, in time, in flexibility and above all gained in freedom. I haven't had to keep a crew member acquainted with my plans. My movements weren't restricted by someone else's temperament, health or knowledge. My decisions aren't weighted by responsibility for another's life. When I learned last night that the weather was improving I had no one to consult; I needed only to order the *Spirit of St. Louis* readied for daybreak. When I was sitting in my cockpit on the muddy runway with a tail wind, there was no one to warp my judgement with a 'Hell let's try it!' or 'It looks pretty bad to me'.

[1]From *The Spirit of St. Louis*, by Charles Lindbergh. Charles Scribner's Sons, 1953.

Unsuccessful tri-motor 'American Legion' of Davis and Wooster.
(Real Photo/Ian Allan)

Lindbergh of course was by no means the Flying Fool, the debonair carefree Lucky Lindy which people were later made to believe, or even 'a lanky demon of the air from the wide open spaces'. The truth was very different, for in spite of his youthful good looks and clean American-boy appearances he was an experienced and hardened pilot, with 2000 flying hours in his log and four escapes by parachute with many other voluntary jumps. Although only twenty-five when he achieved fame he had already been through the rigours of barnstorming, Army training as an officer of the Reserve and the gruelling job of piloting mail planes between St. Louis and Chicago by night and by day and in all weathers. He was also a capable mechanic and well understood navigation. Lucky, perhaps, for any achievement of this sort needs luck but the chances he took, such as reliance on one engine, the decision to fly alone and the deliberate choice to do without a radio or a parachute to save weight were thought out, calculated risks where he made what he thought was the wisest choice.

No, his luck lay more in being the first across while bigger planes and more elaborate organisations who were also after the Orteig prize failed one by one. His plans and organisation were of the simplest, though meticulously thorough and his choice of plane, a small light sturdy monoplane, equally simple and wise.

The Raymond Orteig prize of $25,000 was offered by a French-American who owned the Brevoort Hotel in New York as long before as 1919 for the first non-stop flight either way between Paris and New York. Not until 1926 did this seem a possibility and indeed after Alcock and Brown crossed in 1919 no one succeeded in making a direct flight in an aeroplane across the Atlantic for eight years until Lindbergh in 1927, and after that no one else flew it solo for another five years until Amelia Earhart succeeded after five had failed.

An early failure was the West Indian Jubert Fauntleroy Julian who had set out to try to fly to Ethiopia from New York in 1924 but only got a few yards before crashing. The first serious contender for the big prize was the famous French pilot René Fonck with a crew of four in a three-engined Sikorsky S35 biplane in September 1926. It was fitted with a supplementary undercarriage which was supposed to remain on the ground at take-off. On that day the plane was overloaded and according to one account this was in part caused by the aviators' baggage which included ceremonial dress suitable for their expected welcome. They also carried over 2000 gallons of fuel, enough to carry them for 50 hours for a flight expected to last for 35. At take-off one of the supplementary wheels collapsed, fouled the main undercarriage and the plane crashed. The wireless operator and the mechanic, Islamoff and Clavier, perished in the flames; Fonck and the co-pilot Curtin managed to scramble clear.

As the flying season of 1927 approached two strong competitors for the Orteig Prize were on the scene. First in public esteem was Commander Byrd USN (retired), already famous for his polar flights, who looked like being the first off in April. However, his three-engined Fokker monoplane *America* with Wright Whirlwind

Another unsuccessful competitor for the Orteig prize, the tri-motor 'America' of Commander Byrd.
(Real Photo/Ian Allan)

motors, which was sponsored by Rodman Wanamaker, crashed on its first test flight on landing at Teterboro, N.J., and the plane was seriously damaged, though not wrecked. Byrd broke his left wrist and the intended pilot Floyd Bennet and Noville the co-pilot were more seriously hurt. Antony Fokker, the designer who was piloting, escaped. Byrd's plane was repaired but their departure was held up by over-elaborate organisation and testing so that they got across only after Lindbergh and then with many tribulations, ending up in the sea just off the coast of France after having passed over Paris.

Also in April, on the 26th, there was another fatal crash; Noel Davis and Stanton Wooster, both experienced Navy pilots, being killed on an attempted full-load take-off near Newport News, Virginia. Their plane, a three-engined Keystone Pathfinder biplane *American Legion* with three Wright Whirlwind engines of 225 hp, was half a ton overweight on delivery. In spite of this the pilots were apparently satisfied with the earlier trials with less than full loads.

Lindbergh with the 'Spirit of St. Louis'.
(Associated Newspapers)

Indeed one of their backers, Mr Holt, said to the press: 'Crossing in it from New York to Paris would not be any more venturesome then taking a Pennsylvania train from here (Philadelphia) to New York'. On the fatal day the Pathfinder staggered into the air, failed to gain height, banked to avoid some trees, lost speed and crashed into a swamp, hitting a bank and drowning both men in four feet of water.

Chamberlin and Levine with a single-engined Bellanca monoplane *Miss Columbia* had had troubles too, but after they had created a world record by staying in the air for fifty-one hours in April they seemed likely winners for Lindbergh did not at that stage look a serious competitor. However this team was delayed by mechanical adjustments and bitter arguments and dissension and so also got away after the winner and had to follow his success.

Finally the French pair, Charles Nungesser and François Coli, both most experienced pilots of World War I, in their Lavasseur

162

Lindbergh's arrival at Croydon.
(BBC/Hulton)

single-engined biplane *L'Oiseau Blanc* took off westbound from Paris on 8 May and after crossing the coast were never seen again. Nungesser had been a famous 'ace' in World War I with 45 kills. He was well known and liked in the United States. At first he intended to fly alone and he would have been a most popular winner. However, he selected the almost equally distinguished Coli to go with him. They had accepted the extra risk of a westbound passage because they feared that the Americans mustered in New York would otherwise get away before them. They were great favourites in France and a big crowd had come to Le Bourget to see them leave;

the papers reported evening dress and champagne in the hundreds of motor cars and that M. Levasseur, the designer, kissed them both on both cheeks before leaving. Their plane was overloaded, had a poor outlook, had no radio and no proper compasses; a hazardous enterprise, although the weather was good at the start. Their loss was made more poignant because a journalistic hoax had reported their arrival. The tragedy of Nungesser and Coli lay heavily on all the other competitors and the American Ambassador in Paris, Myron T. Herrick, went as far as to advise the State Department that a successful crossing too soon after their loss would be unwelcome in France and to advise the competitors of this.

As recently as November 1980 *Le Parisien* reported that a Norman restauranteur called Duchemin told his sons on his death bed that he had seen a large white aeroplane half submerged in the sea off Etretat, on the morning of 8 May; it sank before he and his friends could reach it. On reporting the incident at Maritime Headquarters at Fécamp, Duchemin and his companions were sworn to secrecy which he had respected until he lay dying.

As Patrick Dickinson says in his enjoyable book on golf courses: 'There is nothing new to say about St. Andrews, just as there is nothing new to say about Shakespeare'. So too there is nothing new to say about Lindbergh. There are many accounts — there are no fewer than thirteen on this author's bookshelf — and they all say more or less the same thing, all being based it seems on Lindbergh's own account in his book *The Spirit of St. Louis* published long after the event, written in fact between 1938 and 1952. The description of the flight itself occupies 319 pages with his own feelings minutely recaptured and long passages recalling his youth and earlier life.

Some accounts start with his parentage — his father a farmer and Congressman from Wisconsin — others with his grandfather, who was a member of the Swedish parliament and emigrated to the United States at the age of 50. His mother, of British parentage, taught chemistry at a Detroit High School after she was widowed. All accounts agree on Lindbergh's singleness of purpose, his conviction of the importance of flying and his desire to show that a great feat could be attempted and achieved with a minimum of equipment if that were matched by a maximum of effort and skill.

Crowds at Le Bourget.
(Associated Newspapers)

The end of Byrd's flight.
(Illustrated London News)

His simplicity and modesty were also plain to see. He wrote: 'I have never before understood the meaning of temptation or how powerful one's desires can become . . . How could I ever face my partners and say that I failed to reach Paris because I was sleepy'. Not for him the frivolity of the Long Island Aviation Country Club where he would turn his plane away from the idle chatter, as if wishing to blow the caviar into the girls' hair with his slipstream.

After his own account the best and most detailed story of his transatlantic flight is that in the Lindbergh Memorial Lecture[1] given by his friend the late John Grierson, who dramatically died at the Lindbergh fiftieth anniversary celebrations in the United States in May 1977.

Lindbergh, who had long nursed the idea of flying the Atlantic while he was carrying the airmails, got the backing of eight St. Louis businessmen who put up $15,000, which was just enough with careful living to finance him and buy his aeroplane. They looked after the finance while he got on with the flying. After Antony Fokker had refused to sell him a single-engined machine for the attempt Lindbergh decided on a small high-wing monoplane, which was built to his specification in two months by the Ryan Company of San Diego for $6000. It had a span of only 64 ft and an all-up weight of just over two tons, including 450 US gallons of petrol, enough to fly 4250 miles. The engine that he bought to go in his $6000 airframe was a well-known reliable 9-cylinder air-cooled radial Wright Whirlwind J-5C, rated at 223 hp at sea level, making up the total cost of the machine to $10,580. Charles Lanier Lawrance, the designer of this engine, dismissed his dearth of fame by the comment at a Lindbergh celebration dinner years later: 'Who remembers the name of Paul Revere's horse?'.

Although the machine had several attractive advances over the Alcock and Brown equipment, notably a closed cabin, a carburettor

[1]Reprinted in the *Journal of the Royal Aeronautical Society,* October 1975.

heater and a reliable compass — an earth-inductor compass first used by Byrd on his polar flights — the plane was unstable and had to be flown all the time. The pilot could not see forward except through a periscope though in fact he used this only at take-off and landing. At take-off Lindbergh said that it felt more like an overloaded truck than an aeroplane. As Sir Peter Masefield says:

> 'Perhaps the best commentary on Lindbergh's skill came unexpectedly many years later when my son Charles flew the Paul Mantz replica of the *Spirit of St. Louis* at Santa Ana. Asked what he thought of it Charles said: 'I don't want to seem rude but it really is an absolute heap — completely unstable, controls unco-ordinated, ailerons enormously heavy, elevator terribly light, rudder totally ineffective, you can't see where you are going, the engine vibrates like mad and there are hardly any instruments'. Paul Mantz himself agreed it was absolutely hideous to fly and could not understand how they could have gone so far wrong in building the replica. The sequel to this story is quite interesting. Lindbergh himself saw this beautiful replica and asked to fly it for old time's sake. He stayed up for more than hour and when he landed he turned to Paul Mantz and said 'Do you know, I had forgotten just how nice that little aeroplane was! You've got it exactly right, not quite up to modern standards, of course, but it flies just like the old *Spirit* did. It really takes me back, thank you very much indeed[1]'.

Well, whatever it was like, it suited Lindbergh who flew it without trouble from San Diego to St. Louis to show his backers and thence to Curtiss Field on Long Island, New York, arriving there on 12 May to wait for the weather. This was the moment when Lindbergh suddenly appeared as a serious competitor. Curtiss Field was not a suitable aerodrome for an overloaded take-off but Richard Byrd generously offered him the use of the 5000 ft runway at the nearby Roosevelt Field which he had hired for his own attempt. For a week there were reports of storms and fog until on the evening of 19 May there was at last a forecast of improving weather, so next morning at 7.52 am New York time (12.52 pm British Summer Time) after an agonising departure down wind on gluey ground, Lindbergh was airborne. He had had a sleepless night. He said wistfully: 'Even an hour's sleep can separate the 19th from the 20th of May', but he got none.

He had good weather up the New England coast, met a few disturbances over Nova Scotia and passed over St. John's, Newfoundland, a little south of a Great Circle course at midnight

[1] From Sir Peter Masefield's vote of thanks for John Grierson's lecture to the R. Ae. S., from their journal, October 1975.

(BST). A Canadian Pacific liner sighted him about 500 miles out from Newfoundland and the steamer *Hilversum* reported him about 500 miles west of the coast of Ireland going well though he saw neither of these ships.

Still flying by dead reckoning on his Great Circle course, which he followed with extreme accuracy in spite of having to avoid storms, he was sighted again 100 miles off Valentia Island in County Kerry and was seen passing over Smerwick and Baltimore, County Cork. Later he was sighted at St. Germans in Cornwall at 7.40 pm (BST) and by a submarine off Plymouth. Then, in his own words, 'The coast of *France.* It comes like an outstretched hand to meet me, glowing in the light of sunset'. After he was reported at Cherbourg at 8.30 pm this was the signal for thousands to leave Paris for Le Bourget airfield, while 1500 school teachers in the Biltmore in New York stood for a moment in silent prayer. So he landed at 10.22 pm, 33½ hours after take-off, 'amidst scenes of enthusiasm and excitement unparalleled in the world of flying'. This came as a great surprise for he wrote later: 'I'm so far ahead of schedule that I may not find anybody waiting for me on the field'. However, as he said next day, 'I landed perfectly. Then the crowd descended on me and it was all over but for the handshaking.'. His first words were: 'Well I made it'.

As always in Atlantic flying Lindbergh had to contend with some vile weather — storms, fog, high-towering clouds, icing conditions and hours on end of blind flying. But worst of all was the struggle with sleep. Having had no sleep the night before take-off he was struggling with the need to sleep even before night fell on 20 May. But he could not afford to doze for his plane 'would not hold a straight course for two seconds by itself'. All through the night the luminous dials of the instruments had stared at him with cold ghostlike eyes. As dawn broke, he wrote, 'the uncontrollable desire for sleep falls over me in quilted layers . . . This is the hour I have been dreading . . . I know it is the beginning of my greatest test — the third morning since I slept'. To stay awake he kept repeating: 'There is no alternative but death and failure: no alternative but death and failure'. During the long frightful day, fighting sleep and controlling the bucking little aeroplane, the hallucinations of semi-consciousness crept in, spectral ghostly figures in the cabin, voices speaking to him and then hills and trees of an impossible land in mid-Atlantic.

Then at last after 27 hours some fishing boats were seen and then after 28 hours he was truly in sight of land, the coast of Ireland, Valentia Island and Dingle Bay. The temptation then to call it a day must have been enormous but the fatigue fell away, the insatiable desire for sleep disappeared like magic, as did the phantoms and the voices. So he carried on for another 5½ hours to become the most famous flyer in history.

To get the feel of it, it is best to go back to what was said at the time. *Flight* on 2 June 1927 said:

> 'Never in the history of aviation has a flying exploit so stirred the public imagination as the crossing of the Atlantic by Capt. Charles Lindbergh. Probably the nearest approach to it we have had in this country was the return of Hawker and Mackenzie Grieve from their transatlantic attempt in 1919 when, after having been missing for a week, news was at last received that they had been picked up and were safe. Even the successful flight across the Atlantic from Newfoundland to Ireland by Alcock and Brown in the same year hardly aroused such

The Sikorsky S35 of René Fonck.
(Musée de l'Air)

widespread interest and enthusiasm as that which found expression on Sunday last when it is estimated more than 100,000 people flocked to Croydon to see Lindbergh arrive from Brussels'.

The Aeroplane with the pen of C. G. Grey wrote:

'The more sensational newspapers chose to label him 'The Flying Fool' but from all one can gather of his flying career and from what one may judge of his great flight Capt. Lindbergh is an extremely level-headed painstaking pilot who made up his mind to take one almighty big risk for 36 hours in order to achieve world-wide fame. That is not the act of a fool, it is a risk which a brave and ambitious young man is justified in taking at least once in his lifetime.

So far as the flight itself is concerned people may say, and quite rightly so, that it teaches us nothing. We all know that given reasonable luck an engine can run for 36 or 48 or 100 hours without stopping. We all know that an aeroplane could lift enough load to fly for 48 hours without stopping. So given good luck and hoping nothing happens to the 101 little things which may stop an engine there is nothing to prevent anybody from flying the Atlantic. Lindbergh merely backed his luck against the 101 little things . . . But the really remarkable feature of the flight was his navigation'.

Maurice Rostand, son of the dramatist, wrote in verse in *Le Journal* which translated thus: 'You danced all that night and then started at dawn like Alan Seeger[1] . . . It was not great pride in the exploit: it was not even the wishes of two continents that brought you safely here. It was that rendezvous you gave to France's war dead to bow at their tombs'. The reference to dancing all night was perhaps rather unhappy as Lindbergh it is said was later invited to dance by the Queen of England and regretfully had to refuse as he did not know how. Ambassador Herrick telephoned Lindbergh's mother saying: 'Warmest congratulations. Your incomparable son has honoured me by becoming my guest. He is in fine condition and sleeping sweetly under Uncle Sam's roof'.

A hundred thousand people had engulfed him at Le Bourget; a hundred and fifty thousand at Croydon; three million greeted him in New York; he received three-and-a-half million letters, a million telegrams and several thousand offers of marriage. The French Foreign Minister ordered the unparalleled honour of flying the American flag all day over the Foreign Office, the first time such an honour had been accorded to anyone but a visiting monarch. Never again could he call his life his own.

[1] An American who died for France in World War I who wrote 'I have a rendezvous with death'.

Lindbergh bore with great modesty and charm the adulation and the multitude of honours that were heaped upon him but the lack of privacy and the insatiable demands put on him by the public and the press at times made his life almost unbearable until he died at the age of 72. Even before he took off, things were becoming disagreeable and he wrote: 'I'm tired of shaking hands and writing my name of slips of paper and being poked and stared at. I want to spend a normal hour for a change'. He went on to say in his book:

'Up to date my project has been successful beyond my wildest dreams. We've brought the attention to St. Louis that we planned. We've helped focus everybody's eyes on aviation and its future. We've shown what kind of flights a modern plane can make; and my reputation as a pilot had been established. The *New York Times* is going to buy the story of my flight and syndicate it throughout the country. All this is very satisfactory. But there are disturbing elements too. The way the tabloid people acted when my mother came left me with no respect for them whatever. They didn't care how much they hurt her feelings or frightened her about my flight as long as they got their pictures and their stories. Did she know what a dangerous trip her son was undertaking, they asked? Did she realise how many older and more experienced aviators had been killed in its attempt? They wanted her to describe her sensations for their readers. They demanded that we embrace for their cameras and say good-bye. When we refused, one paper had two other people go through the motions and substituted photographs of our heads for theirs — composite pictures they called them. I decided then that I wouldn't write about my flight for the tabloid press no matter what they'd pay me'.

'L'Oiseau Blanc' of Nungesser and Coli.
(Musée de l'Air)

The kidnapping of his child and the subsequent trial and conviction of the murderer added fuel to the fires of publicity from which he was only rescued by a happy married life. To an introverted, reserved man, very much a loner, this extreme inquisitiveness and publicity was an intolerable affront and for a time he lived in England near Sevenoaks to escape it.

After the Paris flight Lindbergh did much for the advancement of flying, starting with a three months' tour of the United States to encourage the construction of airfields and internal air services. Then as technical adviser to TWA and Pan American Airways he carried out long and arduous proving flights in the Arctic and around the Atlantic coasts.

In other ways his involvements were less successful. He became deeply impressed by the strength of Nazi Germany, and if not an admirer at any rate he was bamboozled into accepting an imposing decoration from Goering and after World War II broke out he strove to keep America out of it, as his father had striven to keep America out of World War I. He became an isolationist 'America Firster' speaking out against Lend-Lease and going so far as to say in 1939 that the United States would sooner or later have to demand that Canada should not be involved in the war and so place the USA at risk[1] and to claim in 1941 that it was 'obvious that England is losing the war'. Here he fell foul of President Roosevelt who believed otherwise and attacked Lindbergh's patriotism. When the US was itself attacked, Roosevelt, who like most politicians was not a forgiving man, was not one to change his mind about Lindbergh. So his application to join the Army Air Corps was refused. His war work was therefore with the plane makers, for whom he flew many combat sorties in the Pacific, and no less valuable for that. The old wounds were healed when General Eisenhower appointed him Brigadier General in 1954. His work with Alexis Carrel on aids for heart surgery made him famous in a different sphere. He also became interested in wild-life preservation.

Lindbergh's flight came at the right moment in history. 1927 was indeed a big year in aviation; engines were becoming more reliable with better power-weight ratios; navigation aids were better too. It caught the world's imagination just when long-range flying became reasonably within reach and the style of the achievement appealed mightily to the public. Although his aircraft was of no conceivable use as a passenger carrier, people began to think of possibly travelling by air. Lindbergh foresaw this for he wrote: 'The year will surely come when passengers and mail fly every day from America to Europe,' adding, 'possibly everyone will travel by air in another fifty years'.

The flight too put the American aircraft industry into the front line for the first time. Up until then Britain and France, Germany

[1]Said he: 'But have they (the Canadians) the right to draw this hemisphere into a European war simply because they prefer the Crown of England to American independence'. *Montreal Gazette.*

Lindbergh over England.
(Associated Newspapers)

and Italy, had been the world leaders. Very soon came the American challenge which carried their industry to world supremacy, and who shall deny that Lindbergh did much to bring it about. Just as Francis Ouimet, the young Boston amateur, beat the best professionals in the world to launch the United States into world supremacy at golf in the space of two days in 1913, so Lindbergh in two days in 1927 had an even greater influence on the world.

By the score kept in these chapters Lindbergh may have been only the 92nd man to fly the Atlantic but for all that he became, in the eyes of the world, the first.

14.
The 91 Before Lindbergh

Here in summary is the history of Atlantic flying up to and including Lindbergh's epic voyage in May 1927. The distances and flying times are debatable, depending on whether the whole flight or just the Atlantic passages are quoted.

Successful Flights

Year	No.	Nationality	Pilot & Crew	Aircraft	Route	Date South or North	Distance	Flying Time	Nos.	Cum.
1919	1	US	READ, Stone, Hinton, Breese, Rodd, Rhoads	Curtiss flying boat NC4	Rockaway, Chatham, Halifax, Newfoundland, Horta, Ponta Delgada, Lisbon, Plymouth	8.5.19 to 27.5.19	4096 nm total (North:	53 hr 58 min total West-East	6	6
	2	UK	ALCOCK, Whitten Brown	Vickers Vimy bomber	Newfoundland, Clifden, Ireland	14.6.19 to 15.6.19	1615 nm (North:	16 hr 28 min West-East	2	8
	3	UK	SCOTT, Greenland, Luck, Cooke, Shotter, Harris, Durrant, Maitland, Pritchard, Lansdowne, Mayes, Robinson, Gent, Scull, Ripley, Evenden, Thirlwall, Cross, Gray, Graham, Mort, Northeast, Parker, Watson, Burgess, Smith, Browdie, Forteath, Powell, Edwards, Ballantyne	Airship R34	Edinburgh, Mineola, Long Island	2.7.19 to 6.7.19	3130 nm (North:	108 hr 12 min East-West	31	39
	4	UK	As above minus Ballantyne, Edwards and Lansdowne plus Hemsley, Turner and Angus	Airship R34	Mineola, Long Island to Pulham, Norfolk	9.7.19 to 13.7.19	3314 nm (North:	75 hr 3 min West-East	3	42
1922	5	Portu.	CABRAL, Coutinho	Fairey 'Transatlantic' Mod. Fairey IIID Fairey IIID floatplanes	Lisbon, Canaries, Cape Verde Is., St. Pauls Rocks, Fernando Noronha, Recife, on to Rio	30.3.22 to 17.6.22 to Recife on 5.6.22	1540 nm total (South:	20 hr 15 min total East-West	2	44

Year	No.	Nationality	Crew	Aircraft	Route	Dates	Distance	Time / Direction		No.
1924	6	US	SMITH, Arnold NELSON, Harding	Douglas Cruiser biplane *Chicago* Douglas Cruiser biplane *New Orleans*	Orkneys, Iceland Greenland, Labrador	2.8.24 to 31.8.24	2133 nm Atl section (North:	20 hrs approx East-West	2	48
	8	German	ECKENER, Lehmann, Flemming, Schiller, Pruss, Marx, Speck, Wittemann, Sammt, Scherz, Freund, Ladwig, Siegel, Knorr, Belser, Grozinger, Pfaff, Kiefer, Auer, Thielmann, Christ, Leichtle, Fischer, Thasler, Schwind, Martin, Lang, Steele, Klein, Kraus, Kennedy	Zeppelin LZ 126	Friedrichshafen to Lakehurst New Jersey	12.10.24 to 15.10.24	4345 nm total (North:	80 hr 45 min East-West	31	79
1926	9	Spanish	FRANCO, De Alda, Rada	Dornier Whale flying boat	Huelva, Canaries, Cape Verde Is., Fernando Noronha, Recife and to Buenos Aires		1860 nm Atl section (South:	East-West	5	82
	10	Brazilian	de BARROS, Negrão, Braga, Cinquini	Savoia Marchetti flying boat	Genoa, Canaries, Cape Verde Is., Fernando Noronha, Natal	Started 17.10.26 Crossed: 28.4.27 to 14.5.27	1860 nm Atl section (South:	East-West	4	86
1927	11	Italian	de PINEDO, del Prete, Zacchetti	Savoia Marchetti S55 flying boat	Cagliari to Rabat Bolama, Dakar, Fernando Noronha, Natal and to Buenos Aires	8.2.27 to 24.2.27	2100 nm (South:	27 hrs ap. East-West	3	89
	12	Portu- guese	BEIRES and de Castilho	Dornier Whale flying boat	Lisbon, Portuguese Guinea, Fernando Noronha, Natal	16.3.27 to 17.3.27	1500 nm (South:	East-West	2	91
Not Proven		French	de ST. ROMAN, Mouneyes, Petit	Farman Goliath	St. Louis towards Brazilian coast, piece of aircraft later recovered off Cape Marguarinho	5.5.27	Uncertain (South:	East-West		Not proven
	13	US	LINDBERGH	Ryan monoplane *Spirit of St. Louis*	New York, Paris	20.5.27 to 21.5.27	3125 nm (North:	3½ West-East	1	92

By this reckoning Lindbergh's was the thirteenth crossing of the Atlantic and 91 men had preceded him. Leaving out the South Atlantic the figures shrink to seven flights before Lindbergh and 77 men. Leaving out the airships Lindbergh's becomes the ninth transatlantic flight (North or South) and he the 23rd man.

On the North Atlantic alone, in heavier-than-air craft Lindbergh becomes the thirteenth man across and his the fifth flight, being preceded by Read and the NC4 crew and Alcock and Brown in 1919 and the US Army around-the-world flyers Smith and Arnold and Nelson and Harding in 1924. Counting only direct flights, the NC4 flight with long delays in the Azores and the US Army flights across via Iceland and Greenland come out, leaving only Alcock and Brown ahead.

Finally of course Lindbergh emerges as the first solo flyer of the Atlantic and the pilot of the first flight from mainland America to mainland Europe.

	Flights	Men
In tabular form:		
Total number of successful transatlantic flights before Lindbergh arrived in Paris 21.5.27 and number of men successful	12	91
Airships	3	65
North Atlantic only (all types)	7	77
South Atlantic only (all types)	5	14
Heavier than air, N. Atlantic only	4	12
Direct flights	1	2
Solo flights and mainland to mainland	Nil	Nil

These figures exclude the 'near misses' of de Pinedo's return trip across the North Atlantic and de Saint Roman's 'not proven' attempt to cross from the African mainland to Brazil.

To tabulate the failures is rather more difficult. For example it is hard to know whether the early balloon attempts were attempts or just trial flights. On the whole it seems that many should be omitted like the Suchard airship and Vaniman's airship which blew up in 1912, which leaves only Wellman and his crew and airship as the first to make the attempt.

None of the pre-World War I aircraft can be regarded as having tried nor any flight during the war itself. Even the many efforts to build and fit our aircraft in 1919 for the *Daily Mail* prize or the honour of being First Across cannot readily be categorised as Failures or Untried. The same applies to the Around-the-World attempts, only one of which was successful, though all of them would have had to cross the Atlantic at some stage *en route*. Nevertheless Major Martin and Sgt. Harvey of the US Army Douglas 'World Cruiser' team of 1924 can hardly rank as Atlantic failures as they got no farther than Alaska and the same applies to the British teams of MacMillan and MacLaren in 1922 and 1924, the Portuguese team of Brito Pais, and French of Peletier D'Oisy and the Argentine team of Pedro Zanni.

The winning of the Orteig prize which Lindbergh captured shows up some clearcut attempts which failed but it is not obvious where one should put Davis and Wooster, the Byrd party and Chamberlin and Levine's team. If only as a personal choice here is a list of those who didn't make it, together with those who did:

Year	Leader or pilot	Nation-ality	Aircraft	Where started	Date	Where ended	Remarks
1910	Wellman	US	Semi-rigid airship	Atlantic City, NJ	15.10.10	In the Atlantic	All rescued
1919	Wood	GB	Short Shirl biplane	Holyhead	8.4.19	In the Irish Sea	Rescued; E-W attempt
	Coil	US	Non-rigid airship	St. John's, Nfld.	15.5.19	Lost at sea	Blown from moorings at base
	Read	US	Flying boat NC4	Trepassey, Nfld.	16.5.19	Lisbon	*Made it*
	Bellinger	US	Flying boat NC1	Trepassey, Nfld.	16.5.19	Lost in the Atlantic	Rescued plane lost
	Towers	US	Flying boat NC3	Trepassey, Nfld.	16.5.19	Ponta Delgada Azores	Too damaged to continue
	Hawker	GB	Sopwith biplane	St. John's, Nfld.	18.5.19	Mid Atlantic	Rescued; plane salvaged
	Raynham	GB	Martinsyde biplane	St. John's, Nfld.	18.5.19	At take-off	Crashed on runway; saved
	Alcock	GB	Vickers Vimy biplane	St. John's, Nfld.	14.6.19	Clifden, Ireland	*Made it*
	Scott	GB	Rigid airship R34	Edinburgh	2.7.19	New York	*Made it*
	Brackley	GB	Handley Page V1500 biplane	Harbour Grace, Nfld.	4.7.19	Abandoned attempt	
	Scott	GB	Rigid airship R34	New York	9.7.19	Pulham, UK	*Made it*
1922	Cabral	Portuguese	Three Fairey seaplanes	Cape Verde Islands	18.4.22	Recife, Brazil	*Made it*
1924	Julian	WI	?	New York	4.7.24	Long Is. Sound	Just got off; rescued
	Smith	US	Douglas biplane *Chicago*	Orkney	2.8.24	Labrador	*Made it*
	Nelson	US	Douglas biplane *New Orleans*	Orkney	2.8.24	Labrador	*Made it*
	Wade	US	Douglas biplane *Boston*	Orkney	2.8.24	North Atlantic	Lost at sea; rescued
	Locatelli	Italian	Dornier Whale flying boat	Orkney	10.8.24	Down in North Atlantic	Rescued; plane lost
	Eckener	German	Rigid airship LZ126	Fried-richs-hafen	12.10.24	New York	*Made it*
1925	Casagrande	Italian	Savoia-Marchetti flying boat	Casablanca	3.11.25	At base	Wrecked in in storm

Year	Leader or pilot	Nation-ality	Aircraft	Where started	Date	Where ended	Remarks
1926	Franco	Spanish	Dornier Whale flying boat	Huelva	22.1.26	Recife	*Made it*
	Fonck	French	Sikorsky biplane	New York	21.9.26	At take-off	Crashed at take-off; 2 deaths
	De Barros	Brazilian	Savoia-Marchetti flying boat	Genoa	17.10.26 crossed 28.4.27 to 14.5.27	Natal	*Made it*
1927	de Pinedo	Italian	Savoia-Marchetti flying boat	Cagliari	13.2.27	Buenos Aires	*Made it*

(de Pinedo also crossed the North Atlantic in another plane after Lindbergh had reached Paris)

	Larre Borges	Uru-guayan	Dornier Whale flying boat	Pisa	20.2.27	Wrecked off Sahara coast	Plane wrecked; crew captured; rescued
	Beires	Portu-guese	Dornier Whale flying boat	Lisbon	3.3.27	Natal	*Made it*
	Chamberlin	US	Bellanca monoplane	New York		Ready to fly but beaten to it by Lindbergh, later to Eisleben in Germany	
	Byrd	US	Fokker monoplane	New York	16.4.27	On landing	On test flight

(They later flew the Atlantic after Lindbergh)

	Davis	US	Keystone biplane	Newport News	26.4.27	At take-off	Both killed
	de Saint Roman	French	Farman Goliath biplane	Dakar	4.5.27	Wreckage found off Brazilian coast; flight 'Not Proven'	
	Nungesser	French	Levasseur biplane	Paris	8.5.27	Never seen again	
	Lindbergh	US	Ryan monoplane	New York	20.5.27	Paris	*MADE IT* '

Bibliography

The War In The Air, H. G. Wells. Penguin Books 1908/41.
An Airman's Outings, 'Contact'. Blackwood 1917.
The First World Flight, Lowell Thomas. Houghton Mifflin 1925.
The Boys' Romance of Aviation, Pollard. Harrap 1935.
Wind, Sand and Stars, Saint Exupéry. Harbrace Paper Bound Library 1939.
Historia de la Aeronáutica Española Gen José Gomá Orduña, Prensa Española 1946, 1951.
The Spirit of St. Louis, Charles Lindbergh. Charles Scribner's Sons 1953.
Slide Rule, Nevil Shute. Heineman 1954.
The Flight of Alcock and Brown, Graham Wallace. Putnam 1955.
The Wright Brothers, Fred Kelly. Ballantine Books 1956.
Wings Over the Atlantic, Fore. Phoenix House 1956.
Pathfinder, Donald Bennett. Sphere Books 1958.
Evidence in Camera, Babington-Smith. Chatto & Windus 1958.
Revista do Ar, Aero Club de Portugal. Aero Club de Portugal 1959.
Various papers and journals from the Aero Club de Portugal commemorating the flight of Gago Coutinho e.g. *La Travessia Aerea do Atlantico-Sul* 1922.
Transatlantic Flight Reports by US Navy participants of 1919, US National Archives.
Zeppelins over England, Poolman. Evans Brothers 1960.
This Was Air Travel, Henry Palmer. Superior Publishing 1960.
Claude Grahame-White, Graham Wallace. Putnam 1960.
L'Epopée de Atlantique Nord, Van Hoorebeeck. Centre de Vulgarisation Aereo-Astronautique 1961.
Atlantic Air Conquest, F. H. & E. Ellis. William Kimber 1963.
The Wright Brothers, Gibbs-Smith. HMSO 1963.
Out on a Wing, Miles Thomas. Michael Joseph 1964.
The World's First Aeroplane Flights, Gibbs-Smith. HMSO 1965.
Gago Coutinho, Pinheiro Correa. Pinheiro Correa 1965.
Atlantic Wings, McDonough. Model Aeronautical Press 1966.
The Aeronauts, L. T. C. Rolt. Longmans Green 1966.
Civil Aircraft of Yesteryear, Kenneth Munson. Ian Allan 1967.
Air Atlantic, Alan Wykes. Hamish Hamilton 1967.

I Must Fly, Sheila Scott. Hodder & Stoughton 1968.
The Great Air Race, A. Swinson. Cassell 1968.
Take Off Into Greatness, Grover Loening. Putnam 1968.
Mais Alto, Pinheiro Correa. Aero Club de Portugal 1969.
The First Flight Across the Atlantic, Ted Wilbur. Smithsonian Inst. 1969.
Our Transatlantic Flight, Alcock & Brown. William Kimber 1969.
The Vickers Vimy, P. St. J. Turner. Patrick Stephens 1969.
Sopwith – The Man and His Aircraft, B. Robertson. Air Review Ltd., 1970.
Airships, Robert Jackson. Cassell 1971.
Aeronauts and Aviators, C. Elliot. Dalton 1971.
Barnes Wallis, J. E. Murpurgo. Longman 1972.
First Across, R. K. Smith. Naval Inst. Press 1973.
Cieli e Mari, Cupini. U. Mursia 1973.
The Age of the Airship, Horton. Sidgwick & Jackson 1973.
Airship, Patrick Abbott. Adams & Dart 1973.
The Guinness Air Facts & Feats, Taylor, Taylor & Mondey. Guinness Superlatives 1973.
Fairey Aircraft, H. A. Taylor. Putnam 1974.
Airships, Beaubois. Macdonald & Jane's 1974.
The Schneider Trophy, Mondey. Robert Hale 1975.
The World's Great Pioneer Flights, Capper. The Bodley Head 1975.
History of Aviation, J. W. R. Taylor and K. Munson. New English Library 1975.
Air Transport Before the Second World War, J. W. R. Taylor and K. Munson. New English Library 1975.
Zeppelin and The USA, Hans Knäusel. Luftschiffbau Zeppelin 1976.
Jane's Pocket Book No. 7, Ventry & Kolesnik. Macdonald and Jane's 1976.
The Water Jump, David Beaty. Secker & Warburg 1976.
Pegase, Various authors. Musée de l'Air Oct 1977.
The Blimp Book, Larson. Squarebooks 1977.
Icare, Several authors, Revue de l'Aviation Française 1977.
La Conquète de l'Air 1 & 2, Several authors. Hachette 1977.
The Great Atlantic Air Race, Percy Rowe. Angus & Robertson 1977.
Airshipwreck, Deighton & Schwartzman. Cape 1978.
Flight with Power, Wragg. Barry & Jenkins 1978.
Aviation – The Story of Flight, Several authors. Sundial Publications 1978.
Skywriting, James Gilbert. M. & J. Hobbs 1978.
East Fortune to New York, Bunyan. Museum of Flight 1979.
Air Extra, Cooksley. Ian Allan 1979.
Seaplanes and Flying Boats, Casey & Batchelor. Phoebus 1980.
The Pathfinders, David Nevin. Time-Life Books 1980.
Catalogue of Musée de l'Air, (2 vols).
Mi Vida con Ramón Franco, Carmen Diaz. Editorial Planeta 1981.
Airship Saga, Ventry & Kolesnik. Blandford 1982.

Index